AF652215

Perspectives and Challenges in Indian English Drama

Perspectives and Challenges in Indian English Drama

Edited by

Neeru Tandon

ATLANTIC

PUBLISHERS & DISTRIBUTORS (P) LTD

Published by

ATLANTIC

PUBLISHERS & DISTRIBUTORS (P) LTD

7/22, Ansari Road, Darya Ganj,
New Delhi-110002
Phones : +91-11-40775252, 23273880, 23275880, 23280451
Fax : +91-11-23285873
Web : www.atlanticbooks.com
E-mail : orders@atlanticbooks.com

Branch Office
5, Nallathambi Street, Wallajah Road,
Chennai-600002
Phones : +91-44-64611085, 32413319
E-mail : chennai@atlanticbooks.com

Copyright © Atlantic Publishers and Distributors (P) Ltd., 2006, 2012

All rights reserved. No part of this publication may be reproduced, stored in a retrieval system, transmitted or utilized in any form or by any means, electronic, mechanical, photocopying, recording or otherwise, without the prior permission of the copyright owner. Application for such permission should be addressed to the publisher.

Printed in India at Glorious Printers, A-13, D.S.I.D.C., Jhilmil Industrial Area, Delhi-110095

FOREWORD

Indian-English drama has not been so fortunate as some other branches of Indian Writing in English. As we know, the Indian-English fiction and the Indian-English poetry have established themselves as acceptable forms of writing and western scholars like William Walsh, H.C. Harrex, H.M. Williams Dieter Reiemenschneider and several others have recognized and applauded them as such. But the Indian-English drama remained more or less in a state of hibernation until writers like R.N. Tagore, Sri Aurobindo, T.P. Kailasam, A.S.P. Ayyar, Bharati Sarabhai and Harindranath Chattopadhyaya appeared on the literary horizon and added fresh dimensions and directions to it. Even these dramatists could not succeed in making their plays healthy rivals to those being written in regional languages and holding out a broad-based appeal to the masses. Though the present-day Indian dramatists in English, such as Asif Currimbhoy, Girish Karnad, Badal Sircar, Lakhan Deb, Gurcharan Das, Vijay Tendulkar, and Mahesh Dattani enjoy a sunnier climate and better prospect, it will be pretty difficult for them to rub shoulders with practitioners of other above-mentioned literary forms. These dramatists have however, introduced crisp dialogue and natural expression, new tones and techniques, to render their plays life-like, topical and stage-oriented. Their serious and sustained efforts are bound to yield fruitful results in the foreseeable future.

The present critical anthology on Indian-English drama edited by Dr. Neeru Tandon is a welcome addition to the ever-increasing repertoire of the academic world. It contains some twenty-two papers on diverse authors, themes and trends. The authors treated in it are Girish Karnad, Mahesh Dattani, Badal Sircar, Rabindranath Tagore (chronologically he should have been placed first), and Vijay Tendulkar. The themes dealt with herein are myths and folk-tales, religious propensity, social alienation, audience participation, feminine psyche, role of freedom, and man-woman relationship. And the trends touched upon in this anthology are mythic and symbolic interpretations, focusing on folklore, experimentations in Third Theatre or street plays, and feminist approaches to certain plays. The broad spectrum of Indian-English Drama has also been presented in a few papers. Though a reader may feel the omissions of some eminent dramatists like Sri Aurobindo, Asif Currimbhoy and Gurcharan Das (on whom several researches are being conducted at the moment), no single work can accommodate all of them. In its present shape and size, this anthology will hopefully find a place on the library shelves and enlighten the academics on the perspectives and challenges inherent in Indian-English Drama.

A.N. DWIVEDI
Former Professor of English,
University of Allahabad
&
Presently Senior Consultant in English,
U.P. Rajarshi Tandon Open University,
Allahabad (U.P.)

PREFACE

> Theatre is life. There is no art, no craft, no learning, no yoga, no action, which cannot be seen in it.[1]
>
> —*Bharata's Natyashastra*

Indians are known for their cultural heritage and religious fervour. Their devotion towards their religion and Vedas is exemplary. They considered Drama as 'the fifth Veda.' Being godlike in spirit it could not die even after the Muslim invasion; rather it was absorbed into folk forms in several Indian languages and effortlessly came closer to the common man and his life. The result can be seen in folk forms like *Jatra* and *Nautanki* in Bengal, *Lalita, Khele, Tamasha* and *Dashavtar* in Maharashtra, *Rasadhari* plays in Mathura, *Mohiniattam* and *Kathakali* dance dramas in Kerala, *Bhand Jashn* in Kashmir, *Ramlila* in northern India, *Bhavai* in Gujarat, *Yakshagana, Attadate, Sonnata, Bayalate* in Karnataka, etc. After sometime dramatists paid attention towards plays in modern Indian languages, including English; but surprisingly they were more influenced by English dramatists like Shakespeare, G.B. Shaw and Ibsen than the Indian folk forms. As Girish Karnad admits for his play *Yayati*:

> Oddly enough the play owed its form not to the innumerable mythological plays I had been brought up on, but to western playwrights whom until then I had only read in print: Sartre, O'Neill, and the Greeks...as

1. Adya Rangacharya, *The Indian Theatre* (New Delhi: National Book Trust, 1971) 35.

> there had been no dramatic structure in my own tradition to which I could relate myself.[2]

Perspectives and Challenges in Indian-English Drama brings you twenty-two papers of moderate length, designed to introduce to sincere readers and scholars, India's most important contemporary dramatists Vijay Tendulkar, Badal Sircar, Mahesh Dattani with the established stars like Rabindranath Tagore and Girish Karnad. The idea is to give analytical and critical assessments of their work. It takes into account the contribution of those dramatists who have significantly helped in shaping this genre of Indian-English literature.

For dramatists a play is very obviously a tool for social analysis and thus they appear as spokesperson for their society. Their plays throb nevertheless with strong compassion for their fellowmen and a deep involvement with social and moral issues. Several Indian playwrights show their indebtedness to western thinkers like Sartre, Camus, Pintu or Beckett. But writers like Girish Karnad are conscious of the western norms as well as of the Indian tradition. He has enriched the contemporary Indian drama immensely.

Following the British legacy, theatre as Dramatical device in major cities like Calcutta (East), Madras (South), Bombay (West), Varanasi (North) paved way for modern Indian drama. The translators gave the major help. The translations into English have forged a link between the east and west, north and south and contributed to the growing richness of contemporary creative consciousness, establishing a link between Regional and National theatre. As Girish Karnad admits, "In my childhood, in a small town in Karnataka, I was exposed to

2. Karnad, Girish, *Introduction to Three Plays: The Plays of Girish Karnad*, edited by J. Dodiya, Prestige Books, New Delhi, 1999, 23.

irreconcilably different worlds. Father took the entire family to see plays staged by troupes of professional actors called *natak companies* which toured the countryside throughout the year. The plays were staged in semi-permanent structures on proscenium stages, with wings and drop curtains and were illuminated by petromax lamps."[3] Somewhere he found, "the stage, a platform with a black curtain, was erected in the open air and lit by torches."[4] But very soon *natak* companies and Yakshagana ceased to function. Even when he moved to a big city he could not find a professional theatre over there. As everybody is aware that it is very difficult to make a decent living from theatre only and that is the main reason why it could not become professional. Karnad also supported this point of view by saying, "One was the separation of the audience from the stage and the other was the idea of pure entertainment, whose success would be measured entirely in terms of immediate financial returns and the run of the play."[5]

Another challenge before drama or professional theatre in India was thrown by the film industry, which had learned most of its tricks from the theatre but offered entertainment at cheaper rates. Then language problem was also there as most of the audience chose to ignore it as an unnecessary adjunct. Again in the words of Girish Karnad himself, "The basic concern of the Indian theatre in the post-independence period has been to try to define its 'Indianness.' The distressing fact is that most of these experiments have been carried out by enthusiastic amateurs or part-timers, themselves entirely to theatre. I see myself as a playwright, but make a living in film

3. *Ibid*. 21.
4. *Ibid*. 21.
5. *Ibid*. 24.

and television. There is a high elasticity of substitution between the different performing media in India; the participants—as well as the audiences—get tossed about."[6]

No doubt, in the 1940s so many theatre groups appeared on the Indian cultural horizon, but due to different reasons they failed. During 1980s and 1990s through the translations, Indian-English drama has registered a remarkable growth and maturity. Recently the scenario has started showing different colours. English plays are being staged, especially in the cities like Delhi, Mumbai, Kolkata and Varanasi. Centres like British Council and the American Center arrange troupes from different countries to perform stage show. Other than them, Yatrik group has actively made a significant contribution to the Delhi theatre. Some of the Indian-English plays like Gurcharan Das's *Mira,* Pratap Sharma's *A Touch of Brightness* and Asif Currimbhoy's *The Dumb Dancer* have been staged, but not so much in India as in the other western countries. Its impact may be seen in the syllabus prescribed by various universities where Indian writings in English prescribe novels and poetry originally written in English; but in case of drama, only the translated dramas from regional languages like Bangla or Kannada or Gujarati are prescribed. The reason may be dearth of English plays or their inferiority to regional dramas.

Another significant point that comes into my mind is that number of female dramatists is very less in comparison with the fiction writers. Though Manjula Padmanabhan, Bharati Sarabhai and Dina Mehta are a few contemporary Indian-English playwrights, who can be included amongst the India's best and most serious contemporary playwrights writing in English; they are neither so widely acclaimed nor their plays

6. *Ibid.* 37.

are so frequently being staged. The need of the hour is that Indian dramatists must have the strong desire to locate themselves in their particular Indian contexts, to construct this literary form in between spaces, the desire to critique as well as connect, to show their commitment to their environment, to assert their particular Indianness in the Indian-English dramatic world. Writing now lies very simply in the quality of its genre and the vitality of the tradition, it embodies. Of course it has a long tradition, starting from the Vedic Period, a tradition both of living and of literature, very much alive in writing now, and one would be hard pressed to name another body of writing with quite the same vitality and variety and drive as this genre of literature shows. What editor would not be grateful for the opportunity to publish any or all the dramatists represented here. From an editor's point of view, opportunity is the exact and the right word: it was an opportunity not to be missed and one that I am happy to say was embraced with enthusiasm and gratitude by me. I have been keenly interested in Indian writing in English for the last fifteen years, and the present volume on Indian-English drama is a direct offshoot of this unflagging interest of mine. This book comprises four sections. The first section deals with Indian-English drama in general. This section has four articles regarding the introduction, perspectives, challenges and an overview of Indian-English drama. The second section deals with Girish Karnad as a dramatist and interpretation of his various dramas with his biographical details. It has seven articles in all.

Third section contains three essays on Mahesh Dattani and Badal Sircar. Mahesh Dattani is the first Indian playwright writing in English to be awarded the Sahitya Akademi Award. His play *Tara* is a stage play in two acts, which was first performed as 'Twinkle Tara' at the Chowdian Memorial Hall,

Bangalore, on 23 October 1990 by Playpen Performing Arts Group. The play was subsequently performed as *Tara* at Sophia Bhabha Hall by Theatre Group, Bombay, on 9 November 1991. Last section comprises five essays on Rabindranath Tagore and Vijay Tendulkar; an essay on women playwrights. I tried to supply the biographical details of almost every dramatist discussed here as I personally feel that there is a close connection between life and art.

Three dimensional art of drama, appealing to the visual powers of the audience must be staged, so that it can be enjoyed for its thought content, relevance of the matter clubbed with entertainment and cultural legacy. I invite more attention of the scholars towards other playwrights whose works merit own attention very seriously such as T.P. Kailasam, Bharati Sarabhai, Nissim Ezekiel, Gopal Gandhi, Mohan Rakesh, Manjula Padmanabhan and Dina Mehta. Indian-English drama has acquired a new voice and authenticity too distinct to be ignored. It is keeping pace with the new drama written in English all over the world. A bibliography is provided at the end of the book both by way of acknowledgement and by way of bringing to the notice of teachers and research scholars the material available in the field of Indian drama in English. I hope this volume in the present form would throw fresh light on the approach of the researches in the hitherto neglected field of Indian-English drama.

I take this opportunity to thank Sri Virendrajit Singh (Secretary, Board of Management V.S.S.D. College), Dr. G.S. Nigam, Prof. A.N. Dwivedi, Prof. R.N. Rai, Dr. Vinod Bala Sharma, Dr. R.N. Shukla and Dr. N.M. Nigam for their encouragement and blessings, for continuing guidance and for stepping in with helping hand whenever there were difficulties. Finally, I feel it my duty to express my thanks to my parents and the contributors, and special thanks to my principal Dr. K.K. Tiwari and my colleagues Dr. Supriya Shukla (H.O.D.), Dr. C. Jain, Dr. M. Singh and Dr. R.P. Pradhan in the department whose faith in this enterprise is crucial. I wish to express great appreciation to my husband Sri Sanjay Tandon and my friends Anupam, Surendra and Priya for their loving support, unfailing co-operation and generous helping hand. And lastly, I would like to thank M/s Atlantic Publishers and Distributors for bringing out this book so promptly.

NEERU TANDON

CONTENTS

GENERAL SURVEYS

INDIAN-ENGLISH DRAMA: AN INTRODUCTION

1

Supriya Shukla

Drama being an audiovisual medium of expression has been a very effective and powerful genre in world literature. The birth and development of drama in Greece, Rome, England and India emphasizes upon the fact that it has always been an integral part of culture, highlighting and evaluating moral commitments, religious convictions, philosophical approaches, and social and political changes in various countries. Drama is a mimetic representation of life combining in itself the real and the fictional, art and reality and presenting the events and characters within a dimension of space and time. It combines the qualities of narrative poetry with those of visual arts. It is a narrative made visible,"[1] observes Martin Esslin in 'The field of Drama'.

Hailed as the "Fifth Veda" drama in India has had a rich and glorious tradition. It begins its journey with the Sanskrit plays. "Indian tradition preserved in the *Natyashastra* the oldest of the texts of the theory of the drama, claims for the drama a divine origin, and a close connection with the sacred Vedas themselves,"[2] opines A.B. Keith. The origin of Indian drama can thus be traced back to the Vedic period. It is believed that the dramatic tradition of the ancient Hindus was fully developed even before the Greek drama came to their knowledge. Thus the Hindus of over 2000 years ago had their own theory of drama. With its long history of 2000 years, Indian drama is a unique phenomenon in the literary world.

Indian-English Drama saw the first light of the day when Krishna Mohan Banerjee wrote "The Persecuted" in 1813.

However, the real journey of Indian English Drama began with Michel Madhusudhan Dutt's "Is this called civilization" which appeared on the literary horizon in 1871, though it was not followed by a sustainable creative effort for decades together. After a long hiatus of a few decades it was only by the early 20th century that Indian English Drama gathered momentum under the influence of British Drama. The pre-independence era saw some stalwarts like Rabindranath Tagore, Shri Aurobindo, T.P. Kailasam, A.S.P. Ayyar, Lobo-Prabhu, Harindranath Chattopadhyaya, Bharati Sarabhai, who contributed substantially to the evolution and development of Indian-English Drama. R.N. Tagore and Shri Aurobindo, the two great sage poets of India, were the first Indian dramatists in English worth considering.

Rabindranath Tagore, the awardee of the Nobel Prize for literature and the epitome of Indian spiritual heritage wrote primarily in Bengali but almost all his Bengali plays were translated into English. His best known plays 'Chitra', 'Sacrifice', 'The Post Office', 'Muktadhara', 'The Cycle of Spring', 'The King of the Dark Chamber' are deeply rooted in the Indian ethos and display a unique blend of simplicity and complexity as also conventionality and modernity. Tagore was the first playwright who invested Indian English Drama with symbolic overtones and allegorical significance. Rabindranath Tagore served his fellowmen fruitfully by being an interpreter and mediator between the civilization of the East and the West. Tagore combined the Indian and Western literary traditions to bring a synthesis between the East and the West. Diana Devlin writes "....the philosopher, writer and teacher Rabindranath Tagore set out to unify Indian and European traditions creating plays which have been described as a mixture of Bengali folk drama and Western medieval mystery plays."[3]

Shri Aurobindo was a major Indian-English playwright and an accomplished craftsman in verse. His dramatic genius is revealed through his five complete blank verse plays and six incomplete dramas. Harindranath Chattopadhyaya with his leftist leanings and revolutionary zeal added a new dimension to Indian-English Drama. A.S.P Ayyar wrote six plays and was the next great name in the line of Indian English dramatists. His first play was "In the Clutch of the Devil" (1926) and his last one is "The Trial of Science for the Murder of Humanity." Ayyar's dramas were message-oriented and his plot and characterization were of secondary importance. He used drama as a mode of apprehending reality pertaining to contemporary life.

T.P. Kailasam was another worth considering dramatic voice on the Indian literary scene. He wrote both in English and Kannada. He had a real genius and love for drama. His genius found its full expression in his English plays such as "The Burden" (1933), "Fulfilment" (1933), "The Purpose" (1944), "Karna" (1946) and "Keechaka" (1949). However, he was regarded as the father of modern Kannada drama. G.S. Amur has a very high opinion of T.P. Kailasam and rightly remarks, "A talented actor who appeared in the amateur as well as the professional stage, he brought to the writing of drama an intimate knowledge of the theatre. It is for this reason that his plays whether in Kannada or English have a uniform technical excellence."[4] Bharati Sarabhai was the maiden woman playwright during the colonial era of Indian English Drama who gave Gandhian touch to Indian Drama in English. J.M. Lobo Prabhu was the last great name in pre-Independence Indian-English Drama. Out of the dozen plays which he wrote only two were published before Independence. His "Collected plays" was published in 1956. Lobo Prabhu was adept in writing dialogues and in creating situations though his characters did not appear life-like and convincing to the audience.

In the post-independence era the most prolific playwright Asif Currimbhoy wrote and published more than thirty plays on a wide range and variety of subject matter. History and contemporary politics, social and economic problems, the east-west encounter, religion, philosophy, art were the several issues he wrote on. K.R.S. Iyengar in his own critical framework appreciates the creative calibre of Currimbhoy: "Farce, comedy, melodrama, tragedy, history, fantasy: Currimbhoy handles them all with commendable ease."[5]

Quite a few contemporary playwrights made significant contributions to the development of Indian-English Drama. Pratap Sharma wrote two plays which were staged abroad successfully though they could not be staged in the country. A well established poet, Nissim Ezekiel also enriched Indian-English Drama in his own characteristic way. Being an excellent craftsman his plays reveal and portray his observations of the oddities in human life and behaviour, providing glimpses of a cross-section of contemporary society. However he is best remembered for his poetic creation and not for his dramatic craftsmanship.

Girish Karnad, recipient of Jnanpith award is a living legend in the arena of contemporary Indian-English Drama. His Journey from 'Yayati' to 'The Fire and the Rain' holds a mirror to the very evolution of Indian theatre during nearly four decades. Karnad is India's leading playwright and one of the most outstanding practitioners of performing arts. He is a playwright, actor critic and emissary of Indian art and culture. He is among the foremost media persons of our time. Karnad's achievements as a playwright have received widespread recognition both nationally and internationally. As an actor-director, art-critic and film star Karnad is a man of many achievements though he is at his best in playwriting. He accepts, "I have been fairly lucky in having a multi-pronged career. You know, I've been an actor, a publisher, a film-maker. But in none of these I felt quite as much at home as in playwriting."[6] His five plays 'Tughlaq,' 'Hayavadana,' 'Nagamandala,' 'Tale-Danda' and 'The Fire and the Rain,' have been translated into English, the first two by Karnad himself. His plays are steeped in Indian culture for the themes are taken from myths, legends, folk tales and history, but his approach is modern. He combines classical, folk and western theatrical traditions in his plays. His contribution to Indian-English Drama is immense. Mohan Rakesh, Badal Sircar, Vijay Tendulkar, remained the most representative of contemporary Indian Drama.

The postmodern era seems to be productive for Indian-English Drama as it has received fresh impetus from young writers like Mahesh Dattani and Manjula Padmanabhan. R.K. Dhawan rightly observes: "Very recently Indian English Drama has shot into prominence. Younger writers like Mahesh Dattani and Manjula Padmanabhan have infused new life into this branch of writing."[7] Both Dattani and Padmanabhan project stark realism through their plays. Dattani showcases the mean, ugly and unhappy aspects of human life. The young Bangalore-based Dattani in his early forties is a promising playwright and has won the Sahitya Akademi Award for English literature for his play 'Final Solutions.' Dattani puts drama on a very high pedestal and argues: "Well, I think this is a wrong perception prevailing among the academics, especially the view that writing for the stage is inferior to writing a novel or writing poetry. I think it is important to keep in mind that the playwright is actually a craftsman."[8] "Mahesh Dattani has been acclaimed as a leading playwright in English. Manjula Padmanabhan, another eminent voice in the recent Indian-English Drama has bagged the Onassis Award for her pioneering play 'Harvest' which has been internationally acclaimed. She delineates a dehumanized, terrifying world in which mothers sell their sons for the price of rice. 'Harvest' deals with a miserable family living in a single room in a "Chawl" in Mumbai.

The recent decades have witnessed a spurt of the Indian drama in regional languages and the drama in English translation. Extensive translations of regional plays into English has established a bond between East and West, North and South. However, Indian English Drama has not achieved much in terms of quantity or quality. Compared to all other literary genres its output has been scanty.

The paucity of Indian Drama in English is attributed to several reasons, the first and the foremost being the want of a living theatre. Drama is meant to be staged. The role of the audience is an important factor in the success of a stage show. The study of drama is half literary and half sociological because drama comes in direct contact with the masses, literate as well as illiterate, through, stage production. Thus unless there is a professional stage and encouraging box office prospect there is no incentive to the playwright. It is quite in the fitness of things to quote R.K. Dhawan here: "it is a well-known fact that the real success of a play can be tested on stage. A playwright needs a living theatre to put his work on acid test, evaluate its total effect on the audience and thereby get a chance to improve upon his performance. This handicap has not allowed him to pursue playwriting in a systematic and comprehensive way."[9] Furthermore the form of drama in English still awaits Indianization. The form of the novel, though originally borrowed from the West has got so well assimilated into Indian writings not just in English but even in regional languages that it no longer remains a foreign form. The form of novel and poetry in Indian English are successfully presenting Indian sensibility in a typically Indian style. The form of drama even after attempts made by Girish Karnad to Indianize it by using conventions of Indian classical drama and folk theatre has not been convincingly Indianized.

Besides not many Indian plays get staged. As Rama Sharma in his preface to his "Collected Plays" remark: "Any play written in India in English has an inherent disadvantage in the sense that it is not very often staged. Stage worthiness being a basic test for a play,...? most of the plays written in English do not fulfil this requirement."[10] So plays in English, if they are written at all, are meant to be read, and in turn a writer, who could have been a good playwright turns to other forms, to stories, novels, poetry or essays. As Rama Sharma observes, "However, these can be read and enjoyed for their thought content and for the relevance they have, to the perennial problems of life."[11]

The stunted growth of Indian-English Drama is also due to the inability of Indian playwrights in English to draw upon the rich and varied Indian dramatic traditions and make use of the rich plethora of Indian myth and Indian historical heritage.

However the major hurdle and set back in the development of Indian-English Drama is language. English is not the mother tongue of Indians. It is a 'learnt' language, at best the second language. Natural conversation is the most important aspect of drama but when two Indian characters speak English on the stage, conversation is bound to sound artificial. It fails to create a palpable effect or the required impact on the audience. Only when the characters are shown to belong to the urban elite does a dialogue in English sound convincing. Language is one of the principal determinants of the form of a text. In the process of translation the original form is misrepresented. However, this apparent artificiality in form cannot be dismissed as a mere problem of translation. The artificiality is due to the inherent inadequacy of the English language to express temperaments, sensibilities, and realities which are essentially Indian. A play which is known for its ideas and not its form can be convincingly translated into English as translating idea is not problematic as translating Indian temperaments, mind-sets and sensibilities. English, as Raja Rao pointed out nearly half a century ago, is a language of our intellectual makeup and not of our emotional makeup. Raja Rao could ingenuously overcome this problem by making his characters speak a kind of Indian English as he has done in his novel *Kanthapura*. This can be incorporated in Indian-English Drama.

Moreover, to understand a dramatic performance on stage the spectators do not require a proficiency certificate in that language. That Shakespeare's 'Romans spoke fluent English' and Bernard Shaw's 'St. Joan,' a French girl used English proof of the fact that language cannot be a problem in the creation of dramatic works.

Thus M.K. Naik rightly suggests, "In making his Indian characters speak in English, the playwright needs therefore no qualms at all. Let him first create living characters in live situations, and the language will take care of itself."[12] Besides this, the Indian-English dramatist has to write with a sense of rootedness revealing a true Indian sensibility. He has to overcome the temptation of catering to foreign gallery and blindly imitating the Western models. By doing so the Indian English playwright can effectively overcome challenges and pave the way for a better and brighter future for Indian-English Drama which has survived the test of time and which has all the possibilities and potentialities to carve a niche for itself in the corpus of literary writings in the days to come.

References

1. Martin Esslin, *The Field of Drama.* Great Britain: Metheun, 1987.
2. A.B. Keith, *The Sanskrit Drama.* Motilal Banarsidas, Delhi, 1992, 12.
3. Diana Devlin, *From Mask and Scene: An Introduction to a World View of Theatre.* London, Macmillan, 1989.
4. G.S. Amur, *Kailasam's Quest for Greatness* (Critical Essay on Indian Writing in English). Macmillan, Madras, 1977, 186.
5. K.R.S. Iyengar, *Indian Writing in English.* New Delhi, Sterling, 1995, 732.
6. Girish Karnad, interviewed by Aparna Dharwadker, *Performance, Meaning and the Materials of Modern Indian Theatre.* New Theatre Quarterly, Vol. XI, No. 44, November 1995, 362.
7. R.K. Dhawan, *Flowering of Indian Drama.* Prestige Books, New Delhi, 2004, 24.
8. Sachidanand Mohanty interviewing Mahesh Dattani, *Theatre: Reaching out to People, The Hindu.* New Delhi, February 14, 1999, v.
9. R.K. Dhawan, *20 Years of Indian Writing.* IAES, New Delhi, 1999, 19.
10. M.V. Rama Sharma, *Collected Plays.* Madras, Pearl Publications, 1982, iv.
11. *Ibid.*
12. M.K. Naik, *The Achievement of Indian Drama in English.* Perspectives on Indian Drama in English, 191.

PERSPECTIVES AND CHALLENGES IN INDIAN-ENGLISH DRAMA

2

R.N. Rai

In the world of literature drama is of course the most peculiar, the most appealing and the most delightful of all types of literary pursuits. It is so deeply associated with the inner consciousness of human race that it has rightly been regarded as the best means for the exploration of human nature in all its varieties and manifestations. Since the publication of first Indian English drama *The Persecuted* by Krishna Mohan Banerjee in 1831, more than four hundred plays have been written in English and some of them produced not only in the theatres of India but abroad also. It is, however, to be regretted that the achievement of Indian English drama is not so rich and impressive either in quality or quantity as is that of Indian English poetry or Indian English fiction. When we try to analyse the reasons responsible for its unsatisfactory growth, several factors come to our mind.

First and foremost is the lack of living theatre in our country. As we all know that unlike poetry or fiction, drama is a composite art involving the 'indissoluble relationship between drama and theatre.' As a genre drama can never properly flourish in the absence of its adequate presentation in the theatre. Referring to the uniqueness of drama as a literary form, an eminent Indian critic M.K. Naik in his article "The Achievement of Indian Drama in English" has rightly observed in *Perspectives on Indian Drama in English* (1977):

> Drama is a composite art in which the written word of the playwright attains complete artistic realization only when it becomes the spoken word of the actor on the stage and

through that medium reacts on the mind of the audience. A play, in order to communicate fully and become a living dramatic experience, thus needs a real theatre and a live audience. (180-81)

We find Indian English drama lacking in these essentials which have of course hampered its natural growth from the very beginning till today. Even after the establishment of National School of Drama in Delhi after Independence, so much importance was not given to the performance of English plays as to the development of regional language theatres. In this situation only one or two English plays were being staged every year and these too in the big cities only. Since Indian English playwrights do not have adequate facilities for getting their plays staged in a live theatre, it has done irreparable harm to the growth of Indian English drama. In the forties and after, several theatrical organizations such as Indian People's Theatre, Indian National Theatre, Theatre Unit of Ebrahim Alkazi and the Bhartiya Natya Sangha affiliated to the world theatre centre of UNESCO had been launched, but none of them was exclusively devoted to drama in English. It is a fact worth mentioning that Little Theatre Group which was established as an English Theatre in 1947, was later on switched over to Bengali in 1953. It is a fact that except Gopal Sharma's *Akshara Little Theatre* in New Delhi only an occasional performance of one or two of Indian plays in English used to take place even in big cities like Bombay. Though some of the Indian plays in English like Gurcharan Das's *Mira*, Pratap Sharma's *A Touch of Brightness* and Currimbhoy's *The Dumb Dancer* and *Goa* were successfully staged in the Western Indian-English plays were only occasionally staged very successfully in our Indian Theatres. Even when some plays were staged, they did not evoke widespread enthusiasm nor did they invite 'repeat performances.' The plays like Nissim Ezekiel's *Nalini* and *The Sleep Walkers*, Currimbhoy's *Inquilab* and *The Dolldrummers*, Gieve Patel's *Princess*, Gurcharan Das's *Larins Sahib*, Shiv K. Kumar's *The Last Wedding Anniversary* which have immense theatrical possibilities, had to wait for years for their enactment in theatre. This shows lack of adequate theatrical facilities for the presentation of Indian-English plays. If the playwright is initially conscious of the fact that his play may not be staged at all, he will perhaps allow, says M.K. Naik "his dramatic vision to be insidiously warped in the embryo itself" (185).

There is another problem with the growth of Indian-English drama. English is not the natural medium of communication in our Indian Society. It is spoken and understood only by an elite class in cities or big towns and hence its appeal is confined to the people of this sophisticated class only. It is a well-known fact that they have better source of recreation in the form of Television and Video in their houses and they rarely bother to go to see an English play staged in the theatre.

The entire blame, however, should not be placed upon the lack of adequate theatrical facilities or the difficulty of language as the medium of communication. Even our Indian English playwrights are responsible for their poor performance. They are to be blamed for their ignorance of theatrical requirement for successful presentation of the plays. Drama has had a rich theatrical heritage in our country and it was treated as the 'fifth veda' in our ancient classical literature. In this connection, Adya Ramacharya, one of the pioneers of modern drama in Kannada, advised in his article "Classical Indian Drama and Modern Indian Theatre" to the Indian-English playwrights to "study classical Indian drama and make a re-assessment of it" (41). In the 19th century Bengal only a few notable efforts were made by Michael Madhusudan Dutt who translated his three Bengali plays—*Ratnavali* (1858), *Sermista* (1859) and *Is This Called Civilization?* (1871) into English and by Ram Kinoo Dutt who wrote *Manipur Tragedy* in 1893. In Bombay C.S. Nazir's *The First Parsi Baronet* (1866) and D.M. Wadia's *The Indian Heroine* (1877) are the available examples of Indian-English drama.

In 1875 Madras Dramatic Society was founded, which provided opportunities to amateur Europeans to stage several plays in English. It is however, an acknowledged fact that even by the early part of the twentieth century when theatre movement in different Indian languages had gathered momentum, theatre in English had no chance to develop at all. In the first half of the twentieth century there were three distinguished playwrights—Rabindranath Tagore, Sri Aurobindo and Harindranath Chattopadhyay who made a substantial contribution to the growth of Indian-English drama. Tagore experimented with all categories of plays: five Act plays, poignant tragedies and rollicking comedies, charades, farces and satires, lyrical, philosophical, social and political plays. Out of fifty-three plays only seventeen have been translated—most of them by Tagore himself and others by different reputed translators. It is a remarkable fact that the plays translated by others include some of his most famous plays like *The King of the Dark Chamber* (by K.C. Sen), *The Post Office* (by Dr. Mukhopadhyay), *Mukta-dhara*, *Natir Puja* and *Chandalika* (all by Marjorie Sykes).

Though Tagore kept himself alienated from the professional theatre of Bengal and had hardly any association with the Calcutta stage, he assimilated in his plays several features of Bengali folk drama and Sanskrit drama along with some Western theatrical devices. He never wrote his plays for the common theatre-goers; he rather succeeded in arousing the interest of the enlightened class of people in the experiments he was making. He introduced tragic conflict in many of his famous plays and thus he deviated from classical Indian tradition and moved towards the Western models. One thing, however, is quite obvious that the underlying tone in his plays is one of the harmony and not of irreconciliation. Though deeply rooted in Indian ethos, his plays may be compared to the plays of famous Irish playwright, W.B. Yeats and the 'Belgian Shakespeare'—Maurice Maeterlinck. He was fully acquainted with the ideas of French Symbolist Movement and introduced their methods to the world of theatre. He made an original contribution to the Bengali stage by introducing the symbolic technique which made his plays highly suggestive and meaningful. His famous plays are *Sanyasi*, *The King and the Queen*, *Sacrifice*, *Malini*, *The King of the Dark Chamber*, *The*

Post Office, *Red Oleanders*, *Natir Puja* and *The Mother's Prayer* etc.

Sri Aurobindo was a versatile genius who was not only well versed in the great classics of Greece, Rome, Germany, France, Spain and Italy, but fully acquainted with our rich Sanskrit texts also. He was really a distinguished creative artist with encyclopaedic knowledge of Indian culture, society and metaphysics. In his article on "Sri Aurobindo" published in the *The Times Literary Supplement* (July 8, 1944), D.L. Murray rightly remarked that Sri Aurobindo is "a new type of thinker, one who combined in his vision the alacrity of the West with the illumination of the East." It is, however, an acknowledged fact that the kind of genius Sri Aurobindo displayed in the field of poetry, epic and philosophy, could not be seen in the field of drama. He modelled his plays exclusively on late Victorian pastiches of Shakespearean drama and his characters look like Elizabethan personages in Indian garb. Each time he gave a different tone to the play he wrote: *The Biziers of Bassora* is romantic, *Rodogune* tragic, *Perseus the Deliverer* mythological, *Eric* heroic, *Vasavadutta* legendary. He wrote his five complete plays on a variety of themes which are representative of important culture of the world symbolizing certain significant moments of human history. At the philosophical level Sri Aurobindo deals with the idea of human evolution as is evident from *Perseus the Deliverer* and the idea of love as a benevolent force essential for the restoration of peace and harmony, as can be seen in *The Biziers of Bassora, Eric and Vasavadutta*. In his plays Sri Aurobindo has depicted the perennial clash between good and evil in various forms and presented the heroes as veritable deliverers.

Harindranath Chattopadhyay's plays are serious in tone and spirit. They deal with the brighter and nobler aspects of human life. His *Five Plays* (1929) reveal his socialistic approach towards life. His first play *The Window* deals with the exploitation of textile workers of Bombay by the big industrialists who are curbing their rights ruthlessly. They want to seal their children's mouths and tax even their songs, sobs and laughters. *The Parrot* depicts the woman's urge for freedom from her undesirable husband's bond of marriage. If *The Sentry's Lantern* expresses the agonizing sentiments of three victims, *The Coffin* depicts the crumbling of the bourgeous family. The last important play *Siddhartha, Man of Peace* (1956) provides a viable alternative to the war-torn humanity. The play expresses his deep concern over the discovery of nuclear power and the ensuing crisis in human civilization. His plays, however, failed on the stage on account of his inability to create living characters and moving plots.

There are five other important Indian English playwrights. The first is V.V. Srinivasa Aiyanger who wrote *Blessed in a Wife* (1911), *The Point of View* (1915), *Wait for the Stroke* (1915), *The Bricks Between* (1918), and *Ram Rajya* (1952). A.P.S. Ayyar wrote several plays, some of which are—*In the Clutch of the Devil* (1926), *Sita's Choice* (1935), *The Slave of Ideas* (1941) and *The Trial of Science for the Murder of Humanity* (1942). Ayyar's plays are idealistic and reformistic. Vasudeo Rao wrote a play in five Acts—*Nala and Damayanti* (1928) under the influence of Shakespeare and the Elizabethans. T.P. Kailasam, a powerful Kannada and English playwright, wrote the following plays—*The Burden* (1933), *A Monologue: Don't Cry* (1933), *Karna or The Brahmin's Curse* (1946), and *Keechaka* (1949). In his plays Kailasam has blended both Indian and Western traditions. His *Karna* is the only full length play which has some significant similarities to Sophocle's powerful tragedy *Oedipus the King*. Both *Karna* and *Oedipus* suffer from a fatal curse which shapes their life and destiny. We find a rare, blending of genius and intuitive vision in the plays of Kailasam who has the credit of revolutionizing Kannada drama. Though the theme is based on *Mahabharata*, he is strikingly original in looking at the theme from a new perspective. In his social vision he can be easily compared to Ibsen or Shaw. The last playwright of this period is Bharati Sarabhai who wrote two plays—*The Well of the People* (1943) and *Two Women* (1952) which reveal a distinct impact of Gandhian life-view. *The Well of the People* shows a fine fusion of social awareness with age-old traditional consciousness leading to the emergence of a new outlook. The act of old woman symbolizes the transformation of old India into something new without losing its roots.

The Tagore-Aurobindo-Kailasam tradition of poetic drama continued and flourished after Independence through *Yama and Yami* (1948) by Manjari Isvaran, *Hali* (1950) by G.V. Desani, *Tiger Claw* (1967), *Vivekananda* (1972) and *Murder at the Prayer Time* (1976) by Lakhan Dev and *Rites for a Plebeian Statute* (1969) by Pritish Nandy. Desani's Hali is apocalyptic, symbolic and original. The efforts of Hali and his beloved Rooh are symbolic of the human search for the Eternal and Infinite. The other plays worth mentioning are V.K. Gokak's *The Goddess Speaks* (1948), M.V. Rama Sarma's *Towards Marriage* (1954), *The Carnival* (1960), *Sakuntala* (1975), and *The Mahatma* (1977), Dina Mehta's *The Myth Makers* (1969), Kamala Das's *A Mini-Trilogy* (1971), Manohar Molgonkar's *Line of Mars* (1978).

The other contemporary Indian English playwrights are: Pratap Sharma, Nissim Ezekiel, Gurcharan Das, Asif Currimbhoy, Girish Karnad and Mahesh Dattani. Pratap Sharma's *A Touch of Brightness* (1968), *The Professor Has a Warcry* (1970), Nissim Ezekiel's *Three Plays—Nalini, Marriage Poem* and *The Sleepwalkers* (1969), Gurcharan Das's *Larins Sahib* (1970) are the remarkable plays of late sixties and early seventies. Gurcharan Das has picked up certain events from Indian history, but he has not tried to establish their relationship in the modern context and is just satisfied with the coherent presentation of events.

Asif Currimbhoy is a prolific Indian-English playwright who covers a wide range of themes from history and politics, society and religion, art and metaphysics. Critics differ in their assessment of Currimbhoy's dramatic genius. Whereas Fubian Bowers in his "Introduction" to *The Complete Works of Asif Currimbhoy* considers him "a playwright of international stature" (X), M.K. Naik is of the opinion that 'sheer quantity' in the absence of the 'quality of vision' cannot make him a great dramatist. When, we make an objective assessment of his plays, we realize that he has dramatised human conflict at different levels starting from the flight of Dalai Lama, liberation of Goa, agonies of the people of Bengal to the problems of a Jewish family, English tea planters and Indian Muslims. His famous plays are *The Doldrummers* (1960), *The Dumb Dancer* (1961), *Thorns on a Canvas* (1962), *The Captives* (1963), *The Refugee* (1971), *On Mane Padme Hum!* (1972), *The Dissident MLA* (1974). Through his plays he gives us the message that we are all 'captives' of our own religion, nation, politics, sex, and family. He expresses his deep sense of resentment at the 'seemingly immovable societies around the world.' He has written twenty-nine plays within a short span of little over nineteen years (1956-75).

Currimbhoy deals with the themes of public importance and its variety is amazing. His plays bear ample evidence to this fact that he has a message to deliver, a vision to fulfil. He has the international reputation as a dramatist, as his plays have been performed in several parts of the United States. Though he is aware of the irredeemable absurdities of man, he is always in search of the ways and means for the betterment of human life. He has the unique ability to create visual and auditory images on the stage. With the help of various theatrical techniques he wants to shock the audience and make them feel for the human suffering. He has been constantly experimenting with new forms, new subject-matters, new structures and new modes of presentation.

Like Arnold Wesker he is a social realist and reminds us of Strindberg and Tenessee Williams in the use of his theatrical techniques and stage directions. He is capable of creating proper atmosphere, interesting situations, powerful and animating characters. His plays are poetic, symbolic, passionate, even melodramatic. Sometimes he seems to be interested in creating exciting situations and thrilling incidents rather than delving deep into the ideological and dialectical conflict. Though his plays sometimes suffer from loose plots, sketchy characters, lack of wit and humour and excessive use of documentary elements, they give us the final impression that Currimbhoy is a distinguished playwright and his achievement is both distinctive and impressive.

Modern European playwrights like Shaw, Sartre, Camus, Giradoux and Brecht went back to their myth or history in order to give a message to the contemporary society. Most of the Indian-English playwrights, however, have failed to do so. The only exception in the contemporary era is Girish Karnad who is an impressive actor, intelligent director and powerful playwright, when he started his career as dramatist he had no established theatrical tradition to begin with. The Parsi theatre in spite of its enormous success as a spectacle over nearly seventy years, had produced no significant work. On the other hand the Sanskrit theatre had been an 'elitist phenomenon' even in its glorious days and had restricted itself to a group of wealthy and educated courtiers without having any appeal for the general public. In his "Author's Introduction" to *Three Plays* (1994), Girish Karnad clearly stated:

> To my generation a hundred crowded years of urban theatre seemed to have left almost nothing to hang on to, take off from. And where was one to begin again? Perhaps by looking at our audience again, by trying to understand what experience the audience expected to receive from the theatre. (11)

Girish Karnad was aware of the problems and challenges Indian playwrights had to face after Independence. They had to face a situation in which tensions between 'the cultural past of the country and its colonial past,' between 'the attractions of Western modes of thought and our own traditions' had come out in the open and demanded to be resolved. It is at this point that the famous German playwright and the drama theorist Bertolt Brecht came to his help. Karnad was influenced by certain important aspects of Brechtian theory such as 'alienation effect,' 'interruptive devices,' 'complex seeing,' and 'anti-cathartic effect' but discovered them in his own theatrical tradition. He has the proper understanding of the practical requirements of the theatre and was able to transform any situation into aesthetic experience. He is thoroughly modern in outlook as well as technique. His plays, along with others like that of Badal Sircar in Bangla, Vijay Tendulkar in Marathi, Adya Rangacharya in Kannada, Dharmavir Bharti, Mohan

Rakesh and Shanker Shesha in Hindi have given to Indian dramatic literature, says Nemichandra Jain in his book on *Indian Theatre* (1992), "the status of a creative work" (80).

In his plays like *Yayati*, *Tughlaq*, *Hayavadana*, *Naga-Mandala*, *Tale-Danda*, *The Fire and the Rain*, *Bali* and *Dreams of Tipu Sultan* Karnad uses history, myth, or folk tale in order to reveal and establish modern man's relationship with the past and tackle contemporary problems by placing a continuous parallel between antiquity and contemporaneity. He uses them as metaphors for the expression of contemporary reality. He looks at the contemporary issues with a new perspective and fresh insight and suggests lines of fruitful exploration for Indian-English playwrights. He knows how best Indian stage techniques can be used for creating an 'alienation effect.' He is of the opinion that various Indian dramatic conventions such as the use of Prologue or Epilogue, Chorus, masks, the presence of narrator in the form of *Sutradhara*, *Bhagavata* or *Vachaka*, the seemingly unrelated comic episodes, the mixing of the human and non-human world provide the proper setting for our 'complex seeing,' as in the opinion of Karnad, they "permit the simultaneous presentation of alternative points of view, of alternative altitudes to the central problem" (14). They interrupt the process of emotional identification or empathy on the part of the spectator and create the proper atmosphere for intellectual stimulation which is certainly non-cathartic and hence non-Aristotelian in approach.

Mahesh Dattani, another major English playwright, is rightly regarded by *The International Herald Tribune* as "one of India's best and most serious contemporary playwrights writing in English." Madhu Jain in *India Today* (15 Oct. 1994) "thought of Dattani as an authentic contemporary voice whose plays are rooted in contemporary urban experience." He is not only a director and a playwright but actor, producer and the founder of a theatre group known as *Playpen*. He has the unique capacity to read the rumblings of contemporary urban Indian society and smell the perennial clash between tradition and modernity. He is not interested in polemics but writes frankly about the oppressed or the marginalized class such as minorities, women, gays, hijaras etc. Recognising the importance of Dattani's images taken from the urban middle class milieu, an internationally renowned director, Prof. John McRac, special Professor in the Department of English Studies at University of Nottingham, wrote: "Mahesh Dattani has given us images which could only be created in the theatre, images which deserve to be seen by audiences worldwide, images which give Indian drama a vital new place in modern world theatre" (Quoted by Tanushree Poddar in Society (April, 1995).

Dattani is well acquainted with the works of Tenessee Williams, Arthur Miller and Strindberg. In his dramatic technique he has been compared to Ibsen in the sense that the ghosts of the past, the dark secrets of the human consciousness that torment the present, are explored in his plays in a very subtle and convincing manner. His plays expose the violence of our private thoughts and hypocrisy of our public morals. They draw our attention to the complex prejudices of our class, gender, race and religion in a very subtle and effective manner. They reveal the physical and spatial awareness of Indian theatre on the one hand and the textual rigour of Ibsen and Tennessee Williams on the other.

Theatre is Dattani's life long passion. He is "married to the theatre" and hence he has decided to "cling to bachelorhood" for the rest of his life. His first play *Where There's a Will* was published in 1986 and since 1995 he has been devoting himself fully to the theatrical activities. For the first time in our country in 1998 Dattani set up his own theatre studio meant for the training of new talents in acting, directing and stage writing. In the same year he became the first Indian playwright to receive the prestigious Sahitya Akademi Award for his collection *Final Solutions* and *Other Plays*. In 2000 Penguin Books India brought out an anthology of Dattani's eight plays—*Seven Steps Around the Fire*, *On a Muggy Night at Mumbai*, *Do the Needful*, *Final Solutions*, *Bravely Fought the Queen*, *Tara*, *Dance Like a Man and Where There's a Will* under the title of *Collected Plays*. His latest play *30 Days in*

September came out in 2001. It deals with the sexual abuse of a child and its disastrous impact on man-woman relationship.

In the summer, Dattani engages theatre courses at Portland State University U.S.A. He writes plays for B.B.C. and conducts workshops regularly at his studio and elsewhere. Dattani's studio at Bangalore has now became a renowned center for creative collaboration among playwrights, directors, actors and audience. This is the only place in India where new playwrights can see the different stages in the enactment of their plays and make suitable modifications wherever necessary. Dattani is regarded by reviewers as "an intellectually stimulating playwright" as his plays are "powerfully and brilliantly written." He wants to give more opportunity to the new voices of contemporary era.

There are a few other contemporary Indian English playwrights such as Manjula Padmanabhan, Dina Mehta and P. Sengupta. Manjula Padmanabhan is a powerful playwright and a cartoonist. Her fifth play *Harvest* won the Onassis International Cultural Competitions Prize for theatrical plays in 1997 in Greece. In her another play *Lights Out*. She draws our attention to the heart rendering screams of a woman, Leela which destroy the fabric of domesticity of a middle class couple. Women face violence in many aspects of their daily life. This violence is multi-faceted. It is not merely physical but more often mental and emotional. It is deeply complex, subtle and indirect, hard to recognize and much more difficult to overcome. Dina Mehta's first full length play *The Myth Makers* won an award from Sultan Padamsee Playwriting Competition in 1968 and Tiger, *Tiger* (a play on Tipu Sultan), in 1978 *Brides Are Not Burning* (a play on dowry deaths) won the first prize in a worldwide competition sponsored by B.B.C. in 1979. *Getting Away with Murder* was on the shortlist of seven specially commended radio plays out of 902 entries submitted for the B.B.C. world playwriting competition, 1989. Her other famous plays are *One Plus One Makes Nine* and *Sister Like You*. *Getting Away with Murder* deals with childhood, sexual abuse, infidelity and insecure relationship. It gives an account of three women friends who pass through their own private hells and finally emerge as strangers to one another. P. Sengupta is a columnist, poet, children's fiction writer and above all a playwright. Her first full length play, *Mangalam* won the award for its society relevant theme in *The Hindu*. Her latest play *Keats* was shortlisted for the 1996 British Council International Playwriting Award and won a special commendation. Her play *Mangalam* shows how women have been facing various kinds of violence and abuses for generations. Even then society is moving towards modernity.

We thus see that there is a proper blending of Western intellectual consciousness and Indian theatrical techniques in the experimental plays of contemporary Indian-English playwrights. They deal with the aspirations of the deprived and marginalised sections of society and depict the acute conflicts of contemporary life. Their interaction with the world theatre has broken our alienation from the rest of the world. Indian-English drama can flourish and prosper only when Indian-English playwrights try to imbibe the spirit of rich Indian theatrical tradition and look at different issues with a sense of contemporaneity. Regarding the future scope of Indian-English drama and relevance of Indian theatre I would like to conclude my observation with the remark of our famous playwright, Mahesh Dattani: "I think there is going to be a good positive development, because as we get into the internet age which isolates human beings, the act of communication will be a premium. Theatre is our cultural activity directly related to human beings' communication with each other...."

Works Cited

Jain, Madhu, *India Today*. October 15, 1994.

Jain, Nemichandra, *Indian Theatre*. New Delhi: Vikash Publishing House, 1992.

Karnad, Girish, "Author's Introduction" to *Three Plays*. Delhi: O.U.P., 1994.

Murray, D.L., *The Times Literary Supplement*. July 8, 1944.

Naik, M.K. and Mokashi-Punekar, S., eds. *Perspectives on Indian Drama in English*. Madras: O.U.P., 1977.

Poddar, Tanushree, *Society*. April, 1995.

INDIAN-ENGLISH DRAMA: AN OVERVIEW

3

Vinod Bala Sharma

While trying to initiate a discussion on the 'Perspectives' in Indian-English Drama, we have to first determine the times and situation in which we are trying to review these perspectives.

The perspectives of Indian drama in English are bound by our history, lineage, folk-lore, mythology, social customs, rituals and by our servility to the invaders, first Muslim and then imperialist. These links to the past are important, as they are the roots and soil, which provide nourishment and sustenance to the Indian mind. Reminiscences, nostalgia and retrospection have led sometimes to an imitation of the themes adopted by earlier writers, at other times, the same themes have been recast with a new outlook.

The term de-colonisation is of little relevance in the writing of Indian-English drama, its impact on the Indian dramatic scene was by way of presentation of mostly Shakespeare and to a little extent Shakespeare's contemporary drama and modern writers like Ibsen, Shaw and Wilde. The Western impact gave life to the drying sap of Indian drama leading to the emergence of great writers like Tagore, Harindranath Chattopadhyaya and Sri Aurobindo. These stalwarts made a major contribution to Indian drama. Tagore's hallmark was philosophical complexity conveyed through lyrical simplicity, Aurobindo, carrying forward the tradition of Elizabethan poetic drama and Harindranath Chattopadhyaya brought to India the Marxist theme of the need for economic and social revolution for the upliftment of the dispossessed and the deprived.

The importance of T.P. Kailasham as a dramatist cannot be over emphasized in view of the fact that he chose, in one of his plays, to write on the tragic life of Karna from the Mahabharata.

Post-independence drama in English is at the crossroads where different types of drama stand tall like skyscrapers, posted together but not covering any particular stream. They cannot be labeled together either in theme or style.

On the one side, historical themes have been modified and fashioned by playwrights into forms and styles of their own. Karnad's *Tughlaq,* Tendulkar's *Ghasiram Kotwal* and *Aurangzeb* by Parthasarthi, Mohan Rakesh's heart touching rendering of the *Kalidasa* and Malika Nand and Sundaris' stories in *Arshad Ka Ek Din* and *Lehron Ke Raj Hans,* respectively, are examples.

In other plays, themes are based on the present socio-economic situations, family and marital relations and religious animosities. *Vultures* & *Silence, the Court is in Session* by Vijay Tendulkar are about greed, unscrupulous selfishness and the vulnerable position of women. *Ghasiram Kotwal* though a historical play in so far as it takes historical character and his times as its theme, is also a contemporary play, as Vijay Tendulkar himself claims, because in its culmination it conveys that homicide and genocide, in their most demonic forms, prevail in contemporary society as well.

Girish Karnad picks up themes from Hindu mythology and Kannada folklore. His *Naga Mandala, The Fire and the Rain, Yayati* and *Hayavadna* prove his debt to his Hindu lineage and the rich heirlooms that Kannada folklore has left.

Though rich in tragedy, the Indian mind does not assess the tragic situation in the manner of the west. Except for Vijay Tendulkar we find none of the nihilism and neuropsychological problems that the Western plays are ridden with. Even Badal Sircar who comes closest to the absurdist drama does not denounce life as such, the meaning of life can evade an Indian mind, but his unbound capacity to reconcile paradoxes saves him from the path of absolute degeneration. Badal Sircar's *Evan Inderjit* may find it difficult to solve riddles and Karnad's characters may face the dilemma of the final truth, yet they don't venture into the moral decrepitude and vacuum of Strindberg or Jean Genet. The nearest they come is to Harold Pinter's or John Osborne's characters.

Of all our playwrights, Tendulkar comes nearest to the 'Mega-Death' of moral values. While Bhasa and TP Kailasham associated mega deaths with too strict a code of morality, Tendulkar's version is just the opposite.

The name of Mahasweta Devi cannot be ignored; she being one of the pioneers in writing drama of commitment. I would like however to distinguish between drama touching upon societal issues and drama committed to awakening and arousing public conscience for a wilful change.

Mahesh Dattani and Padmanabhan must be studied as two outstanding playwrights who belong to another category. Both of them write in English and their works are therefore available at hand for the readers of English.

The challenges faced by Indian-English drama have been often talked about. The distance and disparity between the remote and urban population, lack of sponsorship and opportunities to stage plays amongst others. The main challenges are the non-viability of staging plays and the unpredictable response from its viewers. Moreover, cinema and TV are awesome contenders.

An intellectual renaissance in the real sense, and not the pseudo-intellectualism of the bourgeoisie, accompanied by a revolution for literacy may establish drama as one of the most provocative genres of literature and a next-door form of entertainment.

Playwriting and Play staging does deserve an ovation for keeping up its identity amongst a mushroom growth of story telling and poetry.

IT'S A BLOODY STAGE

Alka Saxena

4

Contemporary drama gives a brutal account of the social and political realities. The terse account of the stark realities lays bare the violence of our times. Contemporary drama is generally in the realistic vein. Playwrights are preoccupied with projecting the social and political realities of our time. Many aspects of violence are experienced in our daily lives. Violence in myriad forms has set the stage on fire. It's a bloody stage. This immediately brings to our mind Karnad's play, *The Fire and the Rain*, in which the fire of lust, hatred, anger, envy and treachery brings devastation and murder in cold blood. Modern plays abound in social, familial and political violence. Violence is multifaceted. It is not merely physical; it is mental and emotional, subtle and indirect. Both men and women playwrights have dealt with the different aspects of violence in different ways.

Let us begin by analyzing Mahesh Dattani's play 'Tara.' Dattani's plays have added a new dimension to the accomplishments of contemporary Indian Drama. He occupies a vital new place in modern world theatre. Tara is the story of a woman who is a victim of prejudices imposed by society. The play upholds the conflicts of twins, conjoined at birth, but later separated surgically and emotionally. Tara and her brother are Siamese twins at the time of birth. When the doctors plan a major operation to separate them, it is discovered that the pair has three legs between them. Doctors are of the opinion that the third leg would survive better on the girl and she could be normal, but the boy would need an artificial leg.

But family pressure is brought on the surgeon to give the boy two legs, even after the warning that the boy's body might reject the leg. The surgeon is bribed, but his fears come true. The boy's body rejects the leg and he becomes a cripple. Tara, who could have been a normal girl, is already cripple in order to give the boy a chance. Tara was not given the opportunity to be a normal human being because of gender bias. The inherent preference for the male child, left both of them disabled. When Tara confronts this bitter truth she is extremely hurt. The effect of such extreme violence on Tara's psyche is extremely difficult to overcome.

While dealing with the issue of violence—Body Blows, Women, Violence and Survival—three plays, deserves to be examined. The three plays in this collection portray the victimization of women in Indian society. Different aspects of social violence with reference to women is the chief characteristic of these plays. Manjula Padmanabhan's play *Lights Out* presents the tragic spectacle of the daily rape of women, witnessed at a distance by the middle class characters. These characters are divided on their opinion of this bizarre incident, which has shattered their lives. The crisis of the victim and the brutal description of the torture she undergoes, shakes the audience to the very core. The women onlookers are anguished by the cries for help but the menfolk quieten their conscience by arguing that the victim is probably a prostitute. In real life also we usually are participants of such violent acts but we tend to overlook them.

Dina Mehta's play 'Getting Away with Murder' is more optimistic. The three friends in this play discuss how they have dealt with childhood sexual abuse, infidelity and insecure relations. The men in this play are not silent observers. When Sonali attempts to get even with her molester, she gets the support of her husband and her brother. Physical violence is the subject matter of this intense play. The women characters emerge stronger at the end of the play.

The third play, *Mangalam*, unfolds the issue of abuse and violence that spans generations, and remains constant even though society is supposed to have moved towards development and 'modernity.' *Mangalam* written by Polie Sengupta shows domestic violence in a middle class Tamil Brahmin joint family.

The question of violence and non-violence is superbly handled in Girish Karnad's latest play *Bali—the Sacrifice*. The stage is steeped in blood. The play has been published in 2004. It was commissioned and first presented by the Haymarket Theatre, Leicester, U.K. It portrays the story of a king who is devastated to discover that his queen is involved with a mahout, an elephant keeper. The play opens with the mahout and the queen in a temple courtyard after a sexual interlude. In order to avert the evil consequences of the queen's infidelity, the king is forced to sacrifice a cockerel to the gods. But the king has been converted to Jainism by the queen and so he now believes in non-violence. Therefore, he substitutes a bird made of dough, which in turn has strange results. In the end it is the queen who kills herself. She, by herself is the only true Bali, the sacrifice, in expiation of her sin. Her act becomes the expression of the anger and violence in each one of us.

This brings us to contemplate the incidence of the growing violence around us. Should we sit smugly and accept violence as a way of life? Or can we make efforts to curb it? According to Vijay Tendulkar the occurrence of human violence is not something loathsome or ugly. He believes that violence is a basic quality, it is innate in human nature. He has elaborated on the theory of violence in his project 'Emerging Pattern of Violence.' Violence is triggered by angst in his writing. He has stated "I think anxiety has become part of existence today, triggered partly by the endemic violence. In India, the more we claim we are spiritual people, the more violent we seem to get."[1]

Through *Hidden Fires*, Manjula Padmanabhan attempts to come to grips with the violence of our times. *Hidden Fires* comprises of five powerful hard hitting monologues in which the playwright takes head on issues of violence, intolerance to others and narrow concepts of community and nation. *Hidden Fires* was staged and directed by Arvind Gaur of Asmita theatre in August 2004 in New Delhi. In response to what prompted him to pick up Manjula Padmanabhan's work for solo production, he says "At a time when our society by and large is in flux—with a spate of sectarian violence hitting hard at its heart strings, I could not stop believing in the hard hitting monologues in *Hidden Fires*."[2]

Theatre personality Jayant Kripalani was so moved by these monologues that he staged it in Calcutta with the group The Red Curtain. The five monologues are entitled *Hidden Fires*, *Know the Truth*, *Famous Last Words*, *Points* and *Invocation*. In Invocation the names of ordinary people are used to create a memorial to all those killed by violence for no fault of their own, innocent victims whose names, sometimes have been the sole cause of their death. These monologues came after the 1992 Bombay riots and the more recent Gujarat riots. The solo speaker begins to think of the other deaths that have occurred elsewhere in the world. "The victims of Bangladesh, Srilanka, Afghanistan, Indonesia, Philippines, Cambodia, Congo, North America, South America.... How endless is this list. How heavy with unremembered blood"[3] (Padmanabhan).

It makes us remember the horrors of partition, the Jews of Hitler's Germany—Six million who died in Europe. The memories of violence leave the viewers shaken and thoughtful. The closing lines of Invocation are thought provoking:

> In the names of those who have already died, I make this invocation. Let us be done with violence. Let those who have indulged in violence be named and punished. Let those who have died in violence be named and remembered. With this, I end my invocation.[4]

References

1. Where is the Tradition, Interview *Frontline*, 25 Sept. 1992, 25.
2. Setting the Stage on *Hidden Fires*. Interview *Sahara India*, 14 August, 2004, 34.
3. Padmanabhan Manjula, *Hidden Fires*. Seagull, Calcutta, 2003, 41.
4. *Ibid.*, 40.

GIRISH KARNAD

A BIOGRAPHICAL SKETCH OF GIRISH KARNAD

5

Neeru Tandon

Girish Karnad, undoubtedly, the most important dramatist of the contemporary Indian stage has enriched this genre with his talent as an actor, director, writer, and producer. He has represented India in foreign lands as an emissary of art and culture.

Girish Karnad was born on 19 May 1938 in Matheran, a town near Bombay. He spent his childhood in a small village in Karnataka. In the small town of Svisi, where he grew up; he came in contact with strolling groups of players in 1950s called Natak Mandalis or Natak companies. The seed was sown. After graduating from Karnatak University, Dharwad in 1958, Girish moved to Bombay for further studies. In the meantime, he received the prestigious Rhodes Scholarship and went to England to do his Master's degree. During his stay at Magdalen College, Oxford, Karnad felt immensely interest in art and culture. On his return to India in 1963, he joined Oxford University Press, Madras.

This offered him an opportunity to get exposed to various kinds of writing in India and elsewhere. In 1974, he received an important assignment and was appointed Director of the Film and Television Institute of India, Pune. In 1987, he went to the U.S.A. as fulbright scholar-in-Residence at the Department of South Asian Languages and Civilizations, University of Chicago. From 1988 to 1993 he served as chairman of the Sangeet Natak Akademi (National Academy for the performing Arts), New Delhi. In 1994, he was awarded Doctor of Letters degree by the Karnatak University, Dharwad.

Karnad suddenly found himself as a playwright. When he was preparing to go England; one day as he was reading the

Mahabharata just for fun, he read the story of *Yayati*. Unintentionally he started writing and the result came in the form of a play written in Kannada, the language of his childhood. It was published as a play 'Yayati' in 1961 and later publication of *Tughlaq* in 1964 established Karnad as a master dramatist. Subsequently he published *Hayavadana* (1971), *Angumalige* (1977), *Hittina Hunja* (1980), *Naga-Mandala* (1988), *Tale Danda* (1990) and *Agni Mattu Male* (1995). Girish Karnad wrote all his eight plays in Kannada, these have been translated into major Indian languages including the Hindi. Five of his plays *Tughlaq*, *Hayavadana*, *Naga-Mandala*, *Tale-Danda* and *The Fire and the Rain* have been translated into English. The first three of these have been published by Oxford University Press in India and the remaining two by Ravi Dayal Publishers, New Delhi. Besides his own plays, Karnad has also translated Badal Sircar's *Evan Indrajit* which was well-received in literary circles.

Karnad plays have received an international recognition. These have been widely performed in Europe and America. The play *Tughlaq* has been translated into Hungarian and German. The B.B.C. London, broadcast it in 1979 and Hayavadana in 1993. Directed by E. Alkzi, *Tughlaq* was presented in London by the National School of Drama, Repertory Company as part of the festival of India in 1982. Karnad has received wide recognition for his plays. He got Mysore State Award for *Yayati* in 1962; Kamaladevi Award of the Bharatiya Natya Sangh for the Best Indian Play of the year for *Hayavadana* in 1972; for *Tale-Danda*, he won a number of awards; B.H. Sridhar Award in 1992, Karnataka Nataka Akademi Award for best play of 1990-91 in 1993 and Sahitya Akademi Award in 1994. He has also received Govt. of Mysore Rajyotsava Award in 1970; Sangeet Natak Akademi's Award for play writing in 1972. Award for playwright in 1989; Bookseller and Publisher Association of South India Award in 1992. He has been conferred by the President of India, the Prestigious award 'PADAMSHREE' in 1974 and 'PADAMBHUSHAN' in 1992.

At present Karnad lives in Bangalore with his wife, a medico, and his two children—a daughter and a son.

MYTH AND FOLKLORE IN GIRISH KARNAD'S *THE FIRE AND THE RAIN*

6

N.M. Nigam

Girish Karnad is one of India's leading playwrights. Though he is a Kannada writer yet he has translated his plays in English so as to reach a larger audience. Girish Karnad along with other playwrights Vijay Tendulkar and Rakesh Mohan revived the vogue of theatre. They are trying to uphold the rich cultural heritage of India by using myths and traditional stories in their plays. Karnad has made an effort to fight the legacy of colonialism by upholding Indian values and its cultural ethos. The themes do have contemporary significance but the main focus is on the presentation of complex cultural fabric of India. Karnad loves to discover less known and obscure myths, tries to understand their significance and relate them to the chosen story. Thus he succeeds in providing romantic charm to his plays.

Karnad introduces existentialist issues like identity, split personality, ideological break-ups and dichotomy of life in his plays. His play *Hayavadana* deals with the problem of identity and search for completeness in life. *Nagamandala* focuses on man-woman relationship: the failure of man to treat woman as person and provide space for the fulfilment of her personality. The folk beliefs and the myth of Cobra lend a romantic charm to the story. Tughlaq also deals with dual personality of the king. The ideal and the real are juxtaposed in the play. *The Fire and the Rain* again presents juxtaposition of various ideas and emotions in the background of myths. Folklore and myth move side by side. Karnad writes, "The energy of folk theatre comes from the fact that although it seems to uphold traditional values, it also has the means of questioning these values, of making them literally stand on their head. The various conventions—the chorus, the mask, the seemingly unrelated comic episodes, the mixing of human and nonhuman worlds—permit the simultaneous presentation of alternative points of view, of alternative attitudes to the central problem."[1]

Karnad freely uses masks in his plays. He uses mask in *The Fire and the Rain* also. There are two characters in the play that act as chorus—one is Andhaka who relates the story of Yavakri and the other one is Nittilai. The play within play is a mask play and shows the mixing of human and non human. Arvasu as Vritra—the snake, the manager as Indra, his brother as Vishwarupa. Girish Karnad's views about mask are different from those of western dramatists. The western dramatists interpret mask as two facets of a man's personality: the imposition of another personality on the real one. But Karnad tells that Indian concept of mask is different. To quote Karnad, "...the mask is only the real face 'writ large'; since a character represents not a complex psychological entity but an ethical archetype, the mask merely presents in enlarged detail its essential moral nature."[2]

This myth deals with the battle of Indra with his step brother Vritra. Besides mask Karnad uses myths and folklore in his plays. He dives deep into the archives of ancient scriptures and brings out a scoop full of relevant anecdotes and myths. He ties to find a path in the labyrinthine ways of life with the help of these stories. Karnad picks up the myth but uses only the relevant part of in his plays. He does wonders when he relates these myths to the facts of life. Myths and mask provide a rich texture to his plays and at the same time enhance the knowledge of the viewers about our ancient scriptures. The genius of Karnad lies in the fact that he does not use the full story in the play but picks up only the required part of it and tries to find solutions of the riddle of life through them. The use of myth and folklore provides a rich texture to his plays. *The Fire and the Rain* is full of such myths.

First myth in the play is that of *Indra*—the king of gods and the God of rains. He is also known as 'The Thunder God who conquers the demons of drought and darkness, thus liberating waters....'[3] (the serpent and the son of Tvastri) who is supposed to obstruct water from coming down to earth. According to popular myth, it rains when Indra kills Vritra. Intertwined is the legend of treachery and fratricide. Indra, it is told in the play within play, treacherously killed his brother Vishwarupa. Tvastri gave birth to Vritra so that he could avenge the death of his brother and kill Indra. The myth of Indra, the myth of Yavakri, play within play have been so well knit in the play that they do not appear as three stories but seem to be one single unit.

Karnad uses the mythological story of Yavakri. Yavakri is the son of Bharadwaja, who is considered to be a wise man. Raibhya, the brother of Bharadwaja and himself a saint, overshadows the personality of Bharadwaja and enjoys all the privileges of being a learned man in King's court. This infuriates Yavakri and he decides to go to forest and lead an austere and rigorous life (penance) so as to acquire spiritual knowledge and thereby please Gods. Yavakri completes his penance in ten years and achieves knowledge and power. The aim of Yavakri was to take revenge from Raibhya. Welfare of humanity was not his aim. Knowledge and morality have been treated separately by the dramatist. Tapa (penance) had nothing to do with morality. Yavakri molests the daughter-in-law of Raibhya as soon as he returns. Vishakha, Raibhya's daughter-in-law, had been his flame ten years ago but now she is his cousin's wife. Yavakri takes advantage of her lonely life due to the long absence of her husband Paravasu. Raibhya invokes his evil powers as soon as he comes to know about Yavakri's incestuous deed and the Brahmrakshasas of Raibhya kill Yavakri. The interpretation and symbolic presentation lies hidden in this act—in a draught hit land, Yavakri dies due to the scarcity of water. He could have saved himself had he got a single drop of water in his *Kamandalu*.

As a result Bharadwaja curses Raibhya that he will be killed by his own son. Shocked at his own curse, he suffers from an existential guilt and commits suicide by entering into fire.

Karnad does not blindly follow the mythological story, he deviates from it and manipulates it according to the need of the story. The myth says that Paravasu—Raibhya's eldest son and the chief priest of the Fire sacrifice unintentionally killed his father, taking him to be a wild animal, but in the play Paravasu kills his father intentionally. He believed that his father was responsible for the poor condition of his wife. The dramatist also insinuates that Raibhya had sent his son for the rituals of Fire sacrifice for several years intentionally.

Yajna or Fire sacrifice is a traditional belief. A fire sacrifice is organized to please the god of rains. The king gets a platform built which is called the sanctum sanctorum and nobody except a Brahmin or an upper-caste is allowed to enter the holy area. It is believed that priests do not leave the holy precincts and do not talk to the *shudras* and also do not indulge in sensual pleasures.

The dramatist, through the play, hits at the prevailing social conditions of the period. Society, it is seen, was suffering from the crises of moral values. Caste system was prevalent. Knowledge of Vedas and other scriptures was denied to *Shudras*. The courtier, who comes as messenger of the actor-manager, says: 'He'll make submission from a distance.'[4]

'Please face away from the sacrificial enclosure so you don't pollute it.'[5]

The actor manager requests for the enactment of the play. He tries to justify: "So if Indra is to be pleased and bring to an end this long drought which ravages our land a fire—sacrifice is not enough. A play has to be performed along with it. If we offer him entertainment in addition to the oblations, the god may grant us the rains we're praying for."[6]

The story of *Natya*—the art of dramatics is also a mythological one. Brahma—the father of Indra is said to be the originator of the art of drama. He handed over the art to his son Indra who in turn gave it to a mortal named Bharat. Hence the importance of drama to please Indra. Another justification of holding a play in between a Yajna was that these used to continue for several years, hence the intervals were filled by enacting these plays or by narrating tales. The tales of the great epic *Mahabharata* were told during such intervals only.[7]

The genius of Karnad lies in the fact that he uses these myths and weaves them into a spell-binding modern play. Along with myths and folk tales he mixes issues relating to human existence. Love and hate; trust and treachery; penance and unethical conduct; power and weakness; sacrifice and murder are juxtaposed to each other in the play. There is fire of jealousy, lust and incest in the play *vis-à-vis* the rain of pure love. Nittilai represents pure and sterling qualities of human life—love, sympathy, sacrifice, giving and sharing. Whereas Gods and Brahmins represent treachery and evil. Nittilai, though an outcaste, is full of human attributes and beauty—in figure, spirit and action. She sacrifices herself for the love of Arvasu. She serves him at the risk of her life. Hers is the true Yajna. She becomes the sacrificial goat. The dramatist himself comments: '...She lies there, her eyes open, bleeding, dying like a sacrificial animal.'[8]

Arvasu rises to divine sphere by granting Moksha to Brahma Rakshasa. Nittilai symbolizes true and selfless love whereas Raibhya symbolizes hatred through and through. He is too proud of his knowledge and not only hates his nephew Yavakri but hates his sons and daughter-in-law too. In turn Paravasu also hates his father.

People, in general, including the king posit their faith in rituals and fire sacrifice. They believe in the benevolence of Gods but on the contrary Yavakri, who had spent ten years of rigorous penance in the forest does not have any faith in the divinity of Gods. By his conduct, he shows that the power acquired by him was an evil one. Yavakri's life itself is an illustration of unethical conduct. He becomes the source of tragedy for the whole family by his immoral act of molesting his cousin's wife Vishakha. He dies, as a result, due to the curse of Raibhya (who invokes kritya) and Raibhya is killed by his own son (as a result of the curse of Bharadwaja). His son Paravasu implicates his brother Arvasu in the murder of his father. He is condemned and treated as an outcaste for having committed Brahminicide.

The play very subtly, insinuates at the prevailing practice of exploitation of the lower class by the upper class Brahmins. The father of Nittilai comments: "...that Brahmins bed their women but hesitate to wed...."[9]

This small dialogue throws light on the atrocities committed on the lower class by the upper class. The Brahmins wielded power and the Shudras obeyed them. For example, the actor manager is asked to speak keeping his face away from the sacrificial platform.

There is an undercurrent of incest, jealousy and struggle for power in the play. The characters strive to achieve the four Purusharthas i.e. *Dharma*, *Artha*, *Kama* and *Moksha*. They do not try to achieve these by ethical means. Rather, they resort to all possible unethical means to achieve them. Hence they fail. Fire-sacrifice and the penance do not yield result in the attainment of Dharma. Yavakri's penance and his search for universal knowledge result in pride, conceit, and revengeful activities. He accepts that his motive behind penance was nothing but to avenge Raibhya. He admits: Indra came to me and said: 'you are ready now to receive knowledge. But knowledge involves control of passions, serenity, objectivity.' And I shouted back 'No that is not the knowledge. That is suicide. This obsession, this hatred. This venom, all this is me. I'll not deny anything of myself, I want knowledge so I can be vicious, destructive!'[10]

There arises no question of Dharma, no welfare motive, hence the accursed end. Raibhya stands parallel to Yavakri in the sense that he too is an epitome of hatred and burns in the fire of jealousy and lust. To quote Vishakha, '...on the other, there is lust. It consumes him. An old man's curdled lust. And there is no one else here to take his rage out on but me.'[11]

The curses seem to be predestined and give a tinge of existentialism to the play. Bharadwaj commits suicide by entering into fire suffering from existential guilt of cursing his brother Raibhya.

Nobody achieves Kama *i.e.* sexual and aesthetic pleasure. Paravasu lives away from his wife and Vishakha leads a dull and dissatisfied life. Arvasu about to marry Nittilai gets stuck up in deaths and gets late. As a result he loses Nittilai. Nittilai, though is unable to marry Arvasu receives fulfilment by nursing Arvasu and by feeding the hungry children of the actor-manager. Hers is the only meaningful existence amongst all other characters who spent their lives searching for its meaning and purpose. Arvasu, without doing any penance, receives a boon from Indra and his innocence, his faith, his selfless love for Nittilai make him rise above all. All efforts to bring rain by traditional means prove futile. The riddle of a meaningful existence remains unresolved.

References

1. Karnad, Girish, *Three Plays*. Pub. Oxford, 1995, 14.
2. *Ibid.*, 13.
3. Brockington, Pub. 1992, 10-11. Cited from *The Fire and the Rain*, Oxford, 1999.
4. Karnad, Girish, *The Fire and the Rain*. Pub. Oxford, 1999, 2.
5. *Ibid.*
6. *Ibid.*, 3.
7. *Ibid.*, 67.
8. *Ibid.*, 58.
9. *Ibid.*, 8.
10. *Ibid.*, 23.
11. *Ibid.*, 33.

THE SYMBOL OF AGNI IN KARNAD'S *THE FIRE AND THE RAIN*

7

Anupam Shukla & Alka Saxena

For thirty-seven years Girish Karnad nurtured the desire to turn the myth of Yavakri into a play. The desire burnt like a flame in his heart ever since he first read the story of Yavakri in C. Rajagopalachari's abridgment of the *Mahabharata*. The play *The Fire and the Rain* is the culmination of Karnad's struggle of thirty-seven years. In the preface to the play Karnad writes "For the next 37 years, I struggled with it, trying to fit all the ramifications of the myth within some sort of a manageable shape" (ix).

The Fire and the Rain illuminates universal themes of love, jealousy and loneliness, and also throws invaluable light on serious philosophic aspects, proving that Karnad's sincere efforts have been amply rewarded. A span stretching over almost four decades spent in contemplating how to transform a myth into a play is like a Yajana—a fire sacrifice itself. Karnad's fine perception and genius prompted him to incorporate the Indra-Vritra legend into the plot. In the notes given at the end of the play Karnad writes, 'I cannot remember when I decided to incorporate the Indra-Vritra legend in my plot.... A myth seems complete in itself and yet lead you on to another myth...illuminating the one you started with' (69).

The action of the play is centred around a seven-year long fire sacrifice designed to persuade the gods to send rains. The play falls in three Acts. In each Act the Fire element is present and needs to be closely examined and appreciated.

The play originally written in Kannada is titled *Agni Mattu Male*. In Karnad's own words, "'Agni' is the Sanskrit word for fire. And being a Sanskrit word, it carries, even when used in Kannada, connotations of holiness, of ritual status, of ceremony, which the Kannada word for fire (benki) does not possess. Agni is what burns in sacrificial altars, acts as a witness at weddings, and is lit at cremations. It is also the name of the god of fire" (63).

Agni is of various types. In Sanskrit and Hindi literature we hear of Viraha-Agni, Kamagni, Dvesagni, Krodhagni, Papagni, etc. The moment Agni is translated into the English word Fire, it does loose that spark, that force and power it carries in Sanskrit. Therefore, while reading the translated word Fire in the play, one should constantly be conscious of the different connotations and the power of Fire. Fire is also one of the five major elements that constitute life. Perhaps it is the agni tatva in human beings, that according to its intensity in each individual, makes him jealous, angry, lustful or passionate by temperament.

The Prologue proclaims that a seven-year long sacrifice is being held to propitiate Indra, the God of rain as it has not rained for ten years. Thus the relation between fire and rain is established at the very beginning of the play. The fire that burns at the centre of the step like brick altar has its own symbolic significance, which will be explained later. The unseen presence of the Brahma Rakshasa, a Brahmin soul trapped in the limbo between death and re-birth is also symbolically important. Three major characters of the play Paravasu, Arvasu and Nittilai are also introduced in the Prologue.

Besides significant developments Act I tells us about the penance of Yavakri. In Andhaka's words Yavakri, the son of sage Bharadwaja did tapasya as, "He was seeking God so he could ask for Universal Knowledge" (9).

Even after ten years of rigorous penance Lord Indra did not oblige. The fire of ambition, originally grew out of jealousy and hatred in Yavakri. According to the myth, Bharadwaja's son Yavakri nursed a grievance against the world for he felt his father did not receive the respect which was his due. In order to overcome his humiliation he did severe tapasya to the extent that he stood in the middle of a circle of fire and started offering his limbs to the fire 'Ten years of rigorous penance. And still Lord Indra would not oblige. Finally, Yavakri stood in the middle of a circle of fire and started offering his limbs to the fire.... And that's when the god appeared to him, restored his limbs, and granted him the boon' (9). Yavakri did not realize that the boon of Gods should not be misused. In fact he should have sacrificed his jealousy, anger, ambition, ego and the strong desire to be the most learned man. Even though he was granted the boon, he knew the limitations of his knowledge. What he gained after ten years was 'some knowledge, but probably little wisdom' (14).

Even after the penance when Yavakri opened his eyes he remembered the exact moment he left Vishakha, ten years ago. He thought of the moment he had come to bid farewell to her. Then she had led him to the grove behind her house where they bid a passionate farewell. 'The sweet sick smell of the jack fruit, the maddening hum of a fly. The smell of your body. Ten years later I opened my eyes and I knew I was hungry for that moment' (14). Ten years later when Yavakri opened his eyes he knew he was hungry for that moment. Thus we have Yavakri, who is burning in the fire of greed, ambition and hatred. The hatred is still in his heart, even though he has done penance. He complains to Vishakha that his father should have been invited as the Chief Priest at the sacrifice instead of Paravasu 'Even in the midst of my austerities I wept when I heard the news' (22).

Vishakha tells him the futility of talking all this now as it is the past and gone but, Yavakri lashes out "the past isn't gone. It's here inside me" (23). He professes that "this obsession. This hatred. This venom. All this is me. I'll not deny anything of myself. I want knowledge so I can be vicious, destructive" (23).

Overcome by hatred and the-fire of lust—the Kamagni and the strong desire to take revenge, he tells Vishakha "It was fortunate that you yielded. If you hadn't, I would have had to take you by force" (23). In the Mahabharata myth Parvasu takes Vishakha by force. In the play the relation between Paravasu and Vishakha is shown to be a childhood attraction and Vishakha yields to Yavakri's seduction. An enraged Raibhya invokes the Brahma Rakshasa who annihilates Yavakri.

The fire that burns Vishakha is also dangerous. After Yavakri left for the jungle to do penance, she was married off to Paravasu, against her wishes. For exactly a year Vishakha was plunged into a kind of bliss she had never known. "It was heaven here and now at the tip of all my senses" (16). But the next year the quest of happiness receded into the background. She tells Yavakri that Paravasu "used my body, and his own body, like an experimenter, an explorer. As instruments in a search. Search for what? I never, knew.... You are still lost in the fragrance of the jack fruit, Yavakri, I have known what it is to grow heavy, burst open, drip and rot to fill the world with one's innards" (16). She too is burning in the fire of loneliness—the virahagni. She looks forward to have her husband home once the seven years of the sacrifice are over. Alone I have become dry like a tinder ready to burst into flames at a breath. The burn things around, me down at the slightest chance..." (16). The chance comes a bit early in the form of Yavakri. After yielding to his seduction, she admits "It's my fault. I shouldn't have yielded to you" (23). When she confronts her husband in Act II, she asks him to do a favour by killing her. Perhaps she wants to free herself from the guilt of having betrayed her husband, by dying at his hands. Vishakha burned in the fire of loneliness, separation from husband and lust.

Raibhya, too, felt humiliated by his own son Paravasu, as he was called to perform the fire sacrifice. Vishakha has been witness to the humiliation felt by her father-in-law. "Something died inside your father the day the king invited you to be the Chief Priest. He's been drying up like a dead tree since then. No sap runs in him. On the one hand, there's his sense of being humiliated by you. On the other, there's lust. It consumes him" (32). Paravasu's rage burning inside him is quietened only after he kills his father Raibhya in Act II. Paravasu felt that Raibhya killed Yavakri to disturb him in the last stages of the sacrifice. According to him Raibhya killed Yavakri not to punish him but to be even with him (Paravasu). "He deserved to die. He killed Yavakri to disturb me in the last stages of the sacrifice. Not to punish Yavakri, but to be even with me. I had to attend to him before he went any farther" (33). Paravasu left the fire sacrifice secretly at night only to be even with his father. The anger and hatred towards his father made him commit as grave a crime as Patricide, Brahminicide. His evil schemes are not yet over. He involves his brother Arvasu in this mess and asks him to perform the rites of penitence. Paravasu has to return in order to complete the sacrifice. He instructs Arvasu to perform the rites, "You. As his son, its your prerogative and your duty. Cremate the body right now. And then concentrate on the penitential rites" (35). Arvasu starts piling wood for the funeral pyre. After performing the rites he goes to the sacrificial area. He is encountered by his treacherous brother the Chief Priest, Paravasu who accuses him of Patricide in front of the king and other Brahmins. Paravasu screams, "Patricide—patricide! What is he doing in these sanctified precincts? Throw him out—out! Demon!" (38). Arvasu is dragged by some brahmins. A dazed Arvasu only asks his brother "But why, Brother why? ...why? Tell me why—please" (38). Paravasu signals for the rites to begin by saying that as the sacrifice approaches its completion the demons come out with the sole aim to disrupt the sacrifice.

Act III opens with Nittalai tending to Arvasu. Nittalai stands for peace, humanity and love. Her tending to a wounded Arvasu is highly symbolic. Arvasu had worshipped his brother but now he is shocked to have been betrayed by him. He feels that if Paravasu can justify his act he'll make him pay "I'll revenge myself on him..." (43). This fire of revenge and hatred is ultimately turned to compassion and for the welfare of mankind in general. This change is brought about by Nittalai's purity and simplicity. She not only tends to the physical and mental wounds of Arvasu but also changes his heart. Nittalai's death is her final sacrifice for humanity. Her death helps in changing Arvasu's vision as well. She tells him that all this revenge is of no use 'where will it end?" (43). She advices him to face his brother not in hatred but through the play. By acting in the play he could take the chance of showing Paravasu how good he is. "I'm sure the play will wash off the fear—the anger" (51). It also means that the play will wash away the fiery anger of Paravasu. And ultimately it does happen, as is portrayed in the Epilogue.

The Prologue begins with the scene at the place where the fire sacrifice is being held. The Epilogue too brings us to the same scene. The troupe of actors are staging the Indra-Vritra legend. The parallel between Indra and Paravasu, Vishwarupa and Aravasu and Vritra and the Brahma Rakshasa is structured skilfully. At the point where Vishwarupa enters Indra's fire sacrifice, he is struck from behind by Indra's thunderbolt. Seeing this being enacted on stage Paravasu jumps to his feet rebuking Indra for his treachery Vritra (played by Arvasu) runs for Indra's life. Vritra is agitated. He is uncontrollable. He grabs a torch in his hand and pulls out a dagger from a guard's belt. He pursues Indra and rushes towards the real sacrificial enclosure. The Actor Manager believes that the mask of Vritra worn by Arvasu has come alive and there will be chaos. There is a stampede and the crowds of villagers start rushing to the burning pavilion. The king calls out to the Chief Priest, Paravasu, and asks what should be done. Paravasu who has been watching the play stoically, gets up and without a word calmly walks in the blazing enclosure. Paravasu went and sat in front of the altar and carried on with the sacrifice. He finally went up in flames while Arvasu stood watching untouched.

Paravasu's entering the sacrificial fire symbolises his atonement. The steps that lead to the fire represent men's steps towards renunciation and final atonement. The steps can only be traversed when man sheds his avarice, arguer, ambition, lust and above all his ego. The fire stands for true knowledge, for the divine, for purity. Fire helps man to burn away his vices and it leads him to the realm of immortality. The mortal fears and vices have to be sacrificed before one surrenders himself to God. The sacrifice was being carried out by a sinner and therefore till his atonement it does not rain. The final offering of Paravasu in the sacred fire makes Indra appear. Indra encourages Arvasu to ask for a boon. The description of the steps that lead to the fire is given in the Prologue. The steps have great symbolic significance as explained above. It is a known fact that when a yajna is being performed the Chief Priest asks the participant to pledge to sacrifice atleast one of their vices and it is said that only then the fruits of yajna can be achieved. Paravasu is guilty and the play enacted by the troupe brings his sins to the fore. He quietly enters the fire to redeem for his sins.

The Epilogue also highlights the role of Nittalai—the tribal girl. She would have married Arvasu but fate had other things in store for her. She is married to a tribal of her own clan. When she hears of Arvasu's plight, she betrays her husband. She runs away from him and after finding Arvasu, tends to him. Although serving Arvasu symbolises her love for humanity yet she has sinned and so must die. She is not scared of death. In fact, she tells Arvasu to play the role of Vritra because even though he is triumphant he chooses death. In the end Nittalai is killed by her husband. He slashes her throat with a knife and she is shown lying there, her eyes open, bleeding like a sacrificial animal.

Karnad's play blends myth and folklore through numerous suggestive symbols. He consistently looks into the past in order to examine the present. This creativity is rooted in the Indian tradition, despite having a strong contemporary relevance. He reflects on contemporary dilemmas. Mahesh Dattani a young playwright has said about Karnad's Nagamandala that he has a historic vision but a contemporary voice, which makes his play universal. This vision is not restricted to Nagamandala alone. It is the hallmark of almost all the plays of Karnad.

In *The Fire and the Rain* too, the dialogues between the Brahma Rakshasa, Indra and Paravasu is a commentary on contemporary evils like patricide, fratricide and adultery. The narrative is taut and the play fraught with unremitting tension, as betrayal, murder and seduction enmesh the characters who live out their destinies in a tumult of elemental passions. With its philosophical underpining, the play illuminates universal themes of love, jealousy and loneliness. Given a choice by Lord Indra, Arvasu, chooses to liberate the Brahma Rakshasa, who was involved for evil by Raibhya. Arvasu does not ask for the boon to bring back to life his beloved Nittalai. Rivalry pinned on hatred anger and lust come to an end with the release of Brahma Rakshasa. The final message for the spectators is that the wheels of time must not be turned back; it is the future and the larger welfare of humanity that matters. What Yavakri could not learn after ten years of penance, what Paravasu the Chief Priest could not comprehend, what Raibhya could not learn despite being a renowned sage was learnt by Arvasu, who was ostracized by the brahmins. He learned the lesson of forgiveness, compassion at the hands of the uneducated hunter girl, Nittalai.

Filled with the spirit of revenge, Arvasu tells Nittalai in Act III, that it will rain blood in the end. But Nittalai tried to calm him by saying "Leave that to the Gods" (43). In the end Lord Indra appears and a transformed Arvasu asks for the liberation of the Brahma Rakshasa. The Brahma Rakshasa is a soul burning in Papagni and Kamagni. It is after much contemplation and in a gradual process of learning that Arvasu attains true knowledge, that makes him ask for the liberation of the Brahma Rakshasa.

When Yavakri stood in penance, Lord Indra had appeared and told him that knowledge could not be mastered through austerities. It comes through experience "knowledge is time, it is space. You must move through these dimensions" (13). Yavakri admits, that after his penance he achieved only a few mantras and some mystical powers. He attained "some knowledge but probably little wisdom" (14). But what Arvasu achieved was wisdom. Lord Indra permits Arvasu to ask for a boon, Arvasu says "Lord I have been an ignorant fool all my life.... But after what I have been through, I am wiser. I can now stop the tragedy from repeating itself. I can provide the missing sense to our lives" (60). Finally he asks Indra to grant Brahma Rakshasa his release. Indra grants the boon and the Brahma Rakshasa cries out in triumph.

All of a sudden it starts raining somewhere, for the people can smell the air blossoming with the fragrance of the wet earth. There is thunder and lightening and it starts raining. The people dance and roll in mud. Rain symbolizes the washing away of evil designs from the heart and the mind. It absolves one of sins, it is life giving. The rain fills the hearts of the famished famine-struck people with fond hope and joy to live. Thus the fire sacrifice brings rain. The various agnis burn away in the final sacrifice and true knowledge prevails.

References

Anees Jung, *Seven Sisters* (Penguin India, 1994), 32, 36.

Anita Desai, *Fasting Feasting* (Chatto and Windus, London, 1991), 22.

Arundhati Roy, *The God of Small Things* (India Ink, New Delhi, 1997), 38.

Girish Karnad, *The Fire and the Rain*, Oxford University Press, New Delhi, 1998. (All references from the book are given in parenthesis).

Goodman, *Quintessence of Literary Essays* (Doaba House Booksellers, Delhi, 1993), 11-12.

India Today (Dec. 15, 1993), 57.

Manju Kapur, *Difficult Daughters* (Penguin India, 1998), 10.

Zide, *In Their Own Voice*, The Penguin Anthology of Contemporary Indian Women Poets (Penguin Books India, 1993), 65.

GIRISH KARNAD'S *THE FIRE AND THE RAIN*: A TEXTUAL INTERPRETATION

M.R. Verma & Sanjay Km. Swarnakar

8

Myths are the eternal source of inspiration for the creative writers. According to Jung, myths are expression of the primordial images in the collective unconscious of man. In the beginning, man had certain experiences and received them in his psyche in the form of images. Since they are the first images, they are called archetypes of the collective unconscious.[1]

Among the modern Indian writers, Girish Karnad may be said to be one of the leading writers who have made the use of myth in their creative works. In his play "Yayati" he found the story of king Yayati from the *Mahabharata* providing a very powerful emotional equivalent to what he desired to communicate. In "Hayavadana" he has made use of the ancient myth of the transposed heads. In "Nagamandala" there is the employment of the ancient folk tale of the naga who loved a woman. Girish Karnad has found myths a powerful vehicle to carry the complex ideas of the modern times. Besides, the use of myths enables him to link the continuity of emotions from the beginning of the civilisation to the present age. Thirdly, he is able to interpret the past in terms of the present and *vice versa*. The following remark of Hazel E. Barnes is relevant in the context of Girish Karnad.

> In a period when values are relatively stable, authors tend to use the classical myths merely allusively, enriching the poetic quality of their work with layers of older connotations. In an age more obviously transitional, there is likely to be more of new interpretations.[2]

The play *The Fire and the Rain* was first staged in Minneapolis, USA in 1994 and was published in 1998 and is the translation of his Kannada play, *Agni Mattu Male* by the writer himself. The action of the play moves round a seven-year long fire sacrifice conducted to propitiate the rain god, Indra, to end a devastating spell of drought. Here is woven a complex story of hurt egos, terror-inspiring spiritual powers that are harnessed only to serve envious ends, and all encompassing love which raises a man above the plane of a mere mortal. In this way through a relatively less known myth of Yavakri and Paravasu from the Mahabharata, Karnad has been able to provide a power and universality to some of the basic human sentiments and emotions.

The myth of Yavakri and Paravasu takes place in the Chapters 135-138 in the "Vana Parva" of the *Mahabharata*. It is stated by the ascetic Lomasha to Yudhisthir the Pandava Prince, when they (the Pandavas) were roaming across the land during their banishment. This story belongs to two sages—Bharadwaja and Raibhya as well as their sons. Although both the hermits were endowed with spiritual powers, it was Raibhya who was appointed the royal priest. He had two sons Paravasu and Aravasu and they were also able priests. The son of the sage Bharadwaja, Yavakri had a complaint against the universe, especially against Raibhya and his sons since he realised that his father had not been accorded the repute and recognition that he had in the real sense. So he went to the jungle in order to do a hard penance to please the king of gods, Indra. As a result of his hard penance, Indra himself presented before him. Yavakri made a request to grant him the knowledge of the Vedas but Indra told him that this kind of knowledge could be acquired over the years from a 'guru' and so asked him to return but he continued with his penance; this forced Indra to satisfy his desire.

After his coming back as he (Yavakri) was proud of his achievement, Bharadwaja warned him against delusions of omnipotence. He specially warned him not to interfere with Raibhya who was known for his fury (anger). His fears, however, proved true as Yavakri one day cornered Raibhya's daughter-in-law and forced her to have sex with him. When Raibhya knew it, he was so furious that he invoked the 'Kritya' spirit. By making oblations of the strands of his hair he invoked two spirits one a 'rakshasa' and another a look-alike of his daughter-in-law and sent him to kill Yavakri when Yavakri was taking his mid-day meal, the female spirit went to him and stole his pot of consecrated water. The 'rakshasa' then pursued him. Yavakri required water to invoke his powers but at every spot water dried up. Ultimately he made efforts to enter his father's hermitage, but the blind man who guarded his father's hermitage, did not allow him and the rakshasa behind him killed him with a trident.

Bharadwaja cursed Raibhya that his own son would kill him and was shocked at his own shortcoming and so he immolated himself. Although Bharadwaja knew that his son Yavakri would meet his end due to his evil deeds, yet his son's death made him uninfluenced by reason and logic. Raibhya's sons Paravasu and Aravasu were conducting a fire sacrifice for the king. One night Paravasu came to his cottage. He mistook his father who was wearing a deerskin for a wild animal and shot him dead with his arrow. When he realised what he had done; he cremated and came back to his sacrificial enclosure. He told his brother about his father's death and asked him to go and perform the penitential rites prescribed for Brahminicide because he could not perform the fire sacrifice alone. Meanwhile he would conduct the sacrifice. Aravasu did the same. But when he came back to the sacrifice, Paravasu asked the king that he should not be permitted to enter the sacrificial enclosure as he was a Brahmin killer.

Though Aravasu made his protest and told everybody that it was a lie and Paravasu had killed his father, nobody listened to him and so he was thrown out by the King's guards. Aravasu went to the forest and prayed to the sungod for help. The sungod obliged him and the king came to know that Aravasu was innocent and it was Paravasu who had killed his father. The king asked Paravasu to go away and invited Aravasu to conduct the fire sacrifice. Later on, the sun god restored Yavakri, Bharadwaja and Raibhya back to life at the request of Aravasu and made Paravasu forget his misdeed. When Yavakri came back to his life, he was rebuked by gods for his flaw and asked to follow knowledge in the right way.

Girish Karnad had come across this myth in C. Rajagopalachari's abridgment of the *Mahabharata* while he was still in college. He was attracted by it and the myth continued to come back to him but it took him more than three decades to shape it into a play. He writes:

> For the next thirty-seven years, I struggled with it, trying to fit all the ramifications to the myth within some sort of manageable shape.[3]

Further he tells in his Notes to the play, "Thirty-seven years is a long time to live with a myth for a company. It inevitably grows and changes with one."[4] In some significant aspects Karnad's story certainly is different from the original myth. Bharadwaja and Raibhya in his story are not just friends but brothers and so their sons are cousins. Karnad makes Yavakri and Vishakha, Raibhya's daughter-in-law, lovers and in this way gives a deviation to the story. In the myth, Raibhya creates a look alike of his daughter-in-law and sends her to facilitate the killing of Yavakri. In the play, Vishakha goes to Yavakri to warn him against the Bramha Rakshasa whom her father-in-law has asked to kill him. She deprives Yavakri of his consecrated water, but the situation this time is different. Raibhya as conceived by Karnad in the play, is completely different from the Raibhya of the myth. In the myth Paravasu kills his father without thinking but in the play he does so knowingly. In the myth Bramha Rakshasa after killing Yavakri goes to live with the female spirit created by Raibhya but in the drama he wants liberation from his state of limbo between life and death. This provides a new dimension to the play. The greatest alteration that Karnad has brought about in the myth is in the character of Arvasu (pronounced in the play as "Arvasu") unlike the myth, Arvasu of the play is not a learned priest. On the other hand, he is a young man of eighteen who loves dancing and acting in the drama, something which was prohibited for Brahmins. Not only that, he is madly in the love with a tribal girl, Nittalai and is bent upon marrying her. Nittalai is a creation of Karnad and through the love of Arvasu and Nittalai he has given meaning to the myth. An important addition to the myth in the play is the story of Indra and Vritra presented through the playlet enacted by the troupe of actors and Arvasu to recreate the priests at the fire sacrifice.

The killing of the demon Vritra by Indra is one of the Archetypal myths of India which appeared for the first time in the *Rigveda* and much later with variations in the *Mahabharata*. It is the *Mahabharata* version of the myth that Karnad uses in the play. In this version Indra, Vritra and Vishwarupa are brothers—all sons of Bramha. Indra feels threatened by the popularity of Vishwarupa and kills him treacherously while Vritra tries in vain to save him. Karnad's incorporation of the Indra-Vritra myth in the play reinforces one of the central themes of *The Fire and the Rain*—the treachery of a brother against another, Karnad says about it:

> The myth can be seen as expressing a deep anxiety which informs the whole of Indian mythology, the fear of brother destroying brother. This fear branches out fully and nakedly in the *Mahabharata* where the bonding of brothers within the Pandava and Kuru clans is as close as the enmity between the cousins is ruthless and unrelenting. In the *Ramayana* the fraternal bonding in the Raghu family Rama and his brothers—expresses another facet of the same anxiety with the betrayals of Sugriva and Vibhishana (interestingly in the cause of the ethically correct side) marking the counter point.
>
> The story of Aravasu and Paravasu fascinated me as unusual variant of this Indian obsession with fratricide and it seemed logical too that Yavakri should be their cousin though the *Mahabharata* does not explicitly say so, I cannot remember when I decided to incorporate the Indra Vritra legend in my plot, but years later, while re-reading the original version I was astonished to find that right at the beginning of the tale of Yavakri, Lomasha mentions that the whole story took place on the banks of a river in which Indra had bathed to cleanse himself of the

sin of killing Vritra! One of the fascinating aspects of dealing with the myths is their self-reflexivity.[5]

The brother hatred theme in *The Fire and the Rain* is incorporated in Yavakri-Paravasu clash though Paravasu is not directly in the conflict and Yavakri meets his end not through Paravasu but Raibhya. Karnad shifts the focus of the conflict from the first generations—that of Bharadwaja and Raibhya—to the second generation that of their sons...by removing Bharadwaja from the scene. In the play, when Yavakri returns from his ten-year long 'tapasya' he finds that his father Bharadwaja is already dead. Whatever Yavakri does; is a calculated move to provoke Paravasu. He is burning with a desire to insult Paravasu and the members of his family. He says to Vishakha:

> Grievances! you do not even flatter me with the word 'hatred.' But it doesn't matter. What matters is that I hate your husband's family. My father deserved to be invited as the Chief Priest of the sacrifice. But that too went to Paravasu, your husband. Even in the midst of my austerities I wept when I heard the news. For I knew father would refuse to take offence. I knew he would go and congratulate Paravasu on the honour, embrace and bless him.[6]

Therefore he fixes everything; his meeting with Vishakha and his sexual act with her. Later he tells her that if she had not agreed with it of her own desire, he would have taken her by force. So this becomes known to everybody he calls Raibhya back a day earlier than his fixed coming back. He even determines the time of his deed and tells Arvasu to meet him particularly at that time. He waits for the challenge from the other side so that he might prove his power by despairing their challenge. It is Raibhya and not Paravasu who accepts the challenge and ruins him.

Girish Karnad has presented Paravasu as the symbol of Supreme egotism who is trying through the fire sacrifice not to seek blessings from Indra but to equal him. He considers Yavakri so mean that he cannot be an object of his hatred. He says to Vishakha:

> One can practice austerities like your fool, Yavakri, to coerce the gods to bend to one's will. Stand in a circle of fire. Torture oneself. So many techniques, all equally cross to make the gods appear. And when they give in what do you do? Extend the begging bowl. Give us rains. Cattle sons. Wealth. As though one defined human beings by their begging I despise it. I went because the fire sacrifice is a formal rite structured. It involves no emotional acrobatics from the participants. The process itself will bring Indra to me and if anything goes wrong, there is nothing the gods can do about it. It has to be set right by a man. By me, that's why when the moment comes, I shall confront Indra in silence. As an equal for that is essential that one shed all human weakness. Be alone, absolutely on ones own to face that moment. Become a diamond, unscratchable.[7]

This statement throws light on the character of Paravasu and gives us a clue to the slaying of his father and his betrayal of his brother. In the myth Paravasu kills his father by mistake because of the curse of Bharadwaja. In the play he does it knowingly. Just before he kills him, Vishakha has been blaming her father-in-law of sexually abusing her so she thinks that due to this accusation he has been killed by Paravasu and tells him that now he will never know whether she told him a lie. In response Paravasu tells her:

> You didn't need to be deserved to die. He killed Yavakri to disturb me in the last stages of sacrifice. Not to punish Yavakri but to be even with me. I had to attend to him before he went my father.[8]

He could not allow anyone to disturb the fire sacrifice which was nearing completion and herein lies the reason of his betrayal of his younger brother who doted on him and who followed blindly whatever he told him. Arvasu is baffled at Paravasu's behaviour and so the only thing that he keeps shouting at the sacrificial enclosure when Paravasu accuses him of Patricide and he is being thrown out by the guards is.... "But, why, Bother, why? Why? Tell me why, please."[9]

In his effort to 'shed all human weakness' and to become a diamond unscratchable, Paravasu loses all human emotions and sentiments that make human beings so lovable and respectable. The Brahma Rakshasa comes to him for his release from his limbo. He explains that since Raibhya had created him, he is his brother but Paravasu is not interested. He tells him that he does not need any more brother.

On the other hand, Aravasu has all those qualities what Paravasu is devoid of. Aravasu has an enthusiasm for life and love for other human beings. At the end of the drama Indra appears before him. He asks him to demand what he wishes. People request Arvasu to ask for rain. Brahma Rakshasa requests him to ask for his release or freedom, he himself desires Nittalai back to life. But when Bramha Rakshasa tells him that his Nittalai would not like life at the cost of someone suffering permanently. Aravasu is deeply influenced. He requests Indra for the release of Brahma Rakshasa and this brings rain to the parched land.

So we can say that it is the interpretation of the myth that any knowledge which does not have the human values like compassion, generosity, proper understanding, goodwill, love and humanity can lead to envious hearts, egos and ultimately all ruin and destruction and that makes *The Fire and the Rain* very important and influential play in the modern time.

References

1. C. Jung, "Archetypes of Collective Unconscious" *20th Century Criticism*, ed., H. West Brook, 130.
2. Hazel, E. Barnes, by A.S. Phand, *Essays on Comparative Literature* (New Delhi: Sterling Publisher, 1984), 110.
3. Girish Karnad, Preface to *The Fire and the Rain* (Delhi: OUP, 1988).
4. **Girish Karnad, *The Fire and Rain*,** 74.
5. *Ibid.*, 68-69.
6. *Ibid.*, 22.
7. *Ibid.*, 31-32.
8. *Ibid.*, 33.
9. *Ibid.*, 38.

GIRISH KARNAD'S *TALÉ-DANDA*: A SOCIO-RELIGIOUS PERSPECTIVE

9

Madhumita Ganguli

Post-Independence drama has opened new vistas both technically and thematically. It is observed that drama written in regional Indian languages, and their English translations have gained a remarkable growth in the recent decades. The translations have forged a link between the East and the West and has contributed substantially to the growing richness of contemporary creative consciousness. Novelty of technique is obvious, the language is trusted to suit the purpose. The regional drama in India is slowly paving the way for a special kind of theatre which absorbs all kinds of theatrical art to give it the shape of a new indigenous theatre. Playwrights like Vijay Tendulkar, Badal Sircar, Mahesh Dattani and Girish Karnad prove to be the torch-bearers of a new resurgence of the contemporary Indian drama. They have made bold innovations and experiments, dealt with themes related to the present social scenario, in an effort to bring about social change, and a social cultural revolution to make the people aware of the need to revamp the present social structure and usher in a renewed and better social system.

Girish Karnad is one of the foremost playwrights of the contemporary Indian stage. He has given the Indian stage a richness that could probably be equated with his talents not only as playwright but also as an actor and a director. He is widely appreciated for his technical experiments, as well as, displaying a wide range of themes and subjects. He merges myth and reality, past and the present; he brings in legendary and historical figures to who are able to carry his message of restructuring the present society. His dramatic creations include among others *Yayati, Tughlaq, Hayavadana, Naga Mandala, Fire and the Rain* and *Talé Danda*. Karnad artistically links up the past and the present in his plays, even when he takes up a legendary or a historical figures like Tughlaq in *Tughlaq*, or King Bijjala and Basavanna in *Talé-Danda*, he relates them to the present times, they hold a contemporary relevance.

The present paper deals with, *Talé-Danda* as a play which calls for humanitarianism—a basic tenet of all religions. The play deals with the problem of caste barriers and its debilitating effect on society particularly in the context of the present times. The play emphasizes the love of humanity and brotherhood of man to accept human-beings as human beings, to give them respect and social status, and not to divide our society into factions on the basis of cast and creed. The paper attempts to analyse the play to show how Karnad deals with the problems of casteism which poisonously seeps in to destroy the peace and harmony within the country. He also shows how certain power-mongers utilize this for their own gains. The *Varnashram Dharma* which was once an ideal system centuries ago became vitiated and a blot on the face of humanity when it started to be distorted. *Talé-Danda* re-examines the relevance of the Varna system of India which was in the past hailed as an ideal one, and later it was reduced to a system of the lower castes to the limit of untouchability and discrimination. *Talé-Danda* carries the message that the religious customs need to be reviewed and re-structured, superstitions and bias of any kind should be removed. There is a need for a classless society for the development of the nation otherwise it would destroy the country. *Talé-Danda* calls for a revolution that would usher in a classless, egalitarian society. Karnad picks up a socio-religious theme and moulds it in a historical-cum-political play to carry the message and to make people aware so that they do away with these ignoble practices as untouchability, segregation and not allowing free mixing and inter-caste marriages. *Talé-Danda* literally means *"to behead"* or *"to destroy"* the practice once and for all, through a revolution aiming at social change. To finish of a system which has lost its importance has become relevant in the present day of technical and scientific advancement, in the age of modernization, where a person's individual qualities recommends him not his caste or class.

In *Talé-Danda* Karnad has given an old historical take a new meaning and significance which is highly relevant in the present context. The play is based on a historical incident which took place in the twelfth century but the issues it raises are extremely relevant to our contemporary society. The play is set in a place called Kalyan, the Hindi translation of *Talé-Danda* is called *Rakt Kalyan.* The play questions the two-thousand year old traditional values of the caste-system. As the caste in India is derived from birth alone and cannot be transferred from one caste to another in any way as reward or anything, it is a closed system. The essential features of the caste system was its hierarchy, restrictions on inter-caste marriages and on eating or living together to the extent of not touching each other. Rabindra Nath Tagore questions this in *Chandalika* where Prakriti, a Chandal girl, says, "A religion that insults is a false religion." In *Talé-Danda* Girish Karnad grapples with this problem. Basavanna says, "Some day this entire edifice of caste and creed, this poison house of Vanashram, will come tumbling down. Every person will see himself only as a human being. 'As a bhakta. As a Sharana.' .... the most terrible crimes have been justified in the name of sensation religion" (39). Basavanna, a poet and social reformer, is King Bijjala's confidant and friend. He is an idealistic man. He gathers around him a number of followers who like him believe in a class-less society. His followers include Brahmins too, like Jayadeva and Madhuvarsa. This movement exhorts people to believe in the idea of "work is worship." Basavanna is supported by the King of Kalyan, Bijjala who is himself a 'Kalachurya'—a barber by birth. The story tells us that five generations back Bijjala's ancestors had served as messengers, later through marriages into royal families. Bijjala himself had married a Kshatriya princess from the Royal family of Hoysalas. In this context Bijjala says:

> "A man's caste is like the skin on his body. You can't peel of the skin, wherever the new skin appears people recognize the skin—the same old skin—same old caste—Kshatriyas, Rajputs, Untouchables, herdsmen—This is the special trait of this earth.... I am sixty-two. In all these years the only people whose eyes did not have a shadow of my caste are *sharanas*, Basavanna and his people." (24)

Bijjala was a feudal lord in Mangalwad with the Chalukya rulers, till he met Basavanna, who was at that time just about twenty years old, but 'his life's philosophy was ready.' Basavanna, made Bijjala realize that King is not '*by birth but by merit*' by the noble qualities of head and heart. Bijjala overthrew the previous ruler, by his prowess and skill at warfare, and become the ruler. It was Basavanna's teaching that aroused him and he achieved what was meant for him, or he would have spent his life entrapped in his caste constraints and never attained great things. The play opens when Bijjala had already ruled for fifteen years as the king of Kalyan and became the victim of the conspiracy of Damodar Bhatt (Queen Rambhavati's priest), Mochanna Kramita (Advisor to the king) and Prince Sovideva (who was being denied the right of being called heir-apparent by his father). The conspiracy succeeds in dethroning the king and grabbing power. They also succeed in thwarting Basavanna's reformist movement and his progressive ideas which rejected idol worship, rituals, class-distinctions, casteism, superstitions, profiteering and other social evils.

Karnad shows that Bijjala, the King of Kalyan was not a 'Kshatriya' by birth; he was a barber by caste. He proved to be a good king who was idealistic and noble hearted which proves that the kingly qualities of noble character and an ideal administrator are not the qualities of Kshatriyas alone. A Kalachurya could also be a good ruler. Bijjala says,

> "In all my sixty-two years, the only people who have looked me in the eye without a reference to my, lowly birth deep in their eyes are the '*sharanas*', Basavanna, and this men; they treat me as a human-being.

> Basavanna, wants to eradicate the caste structure, wipe it off, the face of earth. Annihilate the varna system. ... Look at those he has gathered around him: poets, mystics visionaries. All hard working people form the common stock. They sit together indifferent to caste, birth or station." (15)

Basavanna, as a leader wants to eradicate the caste-system and treat everyone as 'a human-being.' Religion does not discriminate among individuals, all humans are equal in the eyes of God, but the upper caste Hindus did not allow the lower castes Hindus to enter the temples or fill water from the wells. Tortures, mental and physical had been perpetrated, violence, and riots had taken place in the name of religion. The main argument of *Talé-Danda* is to treat everyone as a human-being, to give him equal place and treat them with respect, and kindness. This play exposes us to a society of *'sharanas'*—the people who talk of removing caste barriers and unite into one universal religion of love and brotherhood, to eradicate communalism and factionalism which Karnad himself hated and raised his voice against. Karnad has been a critic of religious fundamentalism in India in the recent years. He publicly condemned the destruction of Babri Masjid in 1992, he is strongly against the threat that fundamentalism poses to secularism and multi-culturalism. Karnad wrote in the preface to *Talé-Danda*, "I wrote *Talé-Danda* in 1989 when the Mandir and Mandal movements were beginning to show again how relevant the questions posed by these were for our age. The horror of subsequent events and religious fanaticism that has gripped our national life today have only proved how dangerous it is to ignore the solutions they offered. Either we change our ideologies or the demon will consume us." The play ends in death and destruction, killing violence and bloodshed, the evil powers overcomes the good ones.

The play advocates the removal of caste-barriers even if there is stiff opposition. Basavanna says "In a state of 'sharana' your caste is dissolved." "A 'sharana' retains his occupation but gives up his caste. Ours is a spiritual brotherhood, a community of experience" (68). In act II we find that

Sheelavanta a cobbler boy, is going to marry Kalavati, a Brahmin girl. The author brilliantly develops this dedicate matter and handles the situation deftly to achieve dramatic heights, emphasizing the importance of inter-caste marriages and women empowerment. The Brahmin girl has no objection to marrying a boy from the lower caste; the boy is some what hesitant.

Fearing a revolt and bloodshed, the king wanted to forbid the marriage, Basavanna was also not willing initially because he thought that "the orthodox will see.... Mingling of castes as a blow at the very roots of Varnashram dharma" (38). Both the boy and the girl are converts to the new 'sharana' faith. However the king "staunched the wrath of the people and invited disaster on his own head" (65). Basavanna gives credit to the king. The wedding procession meets success, but the repercussions are not good.

The high point in the play occurs with the marriage. King Bijjala accepts the marriage though the upper caste Hindus reject it. It signifies a marriage not of love but of ideologies. Even though the families are 'sharanas' the 'inter-caste' alliance is considered in the light of what they were earlier, according to their castes. The caste sticks to them like a second skin, which they cannot tear and throw away. Basavanna, with his pragmatic wisdom tells the 'sharanas' regarding the marriage, "we are not ready for the kind of revolution the wedding is. We haven't worked long enough" (44). Karnad feels that the process is slow, a long drawn out process of social change and not an over night revolution. Basavanna tells the 'sharanas' that they should attend to the little problems of day-to-day life to change their attitude rather than await a major event. He says "they are the challenges a 'sharana' must learn to love" (52).

The upper castes and Brahmins are provoked by the challenge aimed to dismantle their centuries old strong Varnashrama system, they are outraged and condemn the sacrilege of such a profane act of an inter-caste marriage. They put forth clever arrangements reiterating the logic in the caste-order. The chief priest says, "hierarchy which accommodates difference is more humane than equality which enforces conformity" (57).

Damodar Bhatta's conspiracy against the king starts with Sovideva to rise in revolt against his father because the king has failed to stop the marriage and instead he had sided with the 'sharanas.' Damodar Bhatta says, "This marriage is a blow to our Vedic civilization. It takes centuries. Inequality is in nature itself. Struggle, competition and violence are all part of Mother Nature. The varnashram follows this" (64).

King Bijjala is dethroned, but not killed by either Damodar Bhatta or Prince Sovideva, it is left to Jagadev, a Brahmin who had converted into 'sharana' sect. Jagadev enters the palace through a secret passage and kills Bijjalla by enticing him out of the Shiva temple. Basavanna leaves Kalyan, with about seven hundred and seventy 'sharanas.' But there were still over a lakh of 'sharanas' in Kalyan, who were in danger. Sovideva, Damodar and Kramita decide to destroy them. Kramita insists on the decimation of the 'sharanas.' He says, "Maharaj, the Kashmir Emperor Mihirbaba destroyed 1600 Buddha Viharas to stop the Buddhists. You know yourself that our neighbour Tamil Emperor Pandeya got 8000 Jain Minars crushed. Why should we be so contemplative? Why such cowardice?"

The fathers of the bride and groom are caught, their eyes are scooped out, they are tied to the legs of an elephant and are dragged through the streets of Kalyan. The whole city burns. There are widespread riots, stampedes, murders, rapes, looting and destruction. Damodar Bhatta is killed; Sovideva wants complete annihilation of the 'sharanas.' He orders the sharanas to be killed he says "They are snakes destroy them. Don't let them run, pursue them and kill them. Men, women and children.... Don't spare anyone—set the hunting dogs on them. Bushes, forests, houses ever protects the 'sharanas' burn it—Burn their holy books——" (94). The entire city of Kalyan is bathed in the blood of innocent people, in such a power-hungry political set up men and women are just pawns to be sacrificed for self-interest and for power. King Sovideva says, "Women and men of lower castes will have to live within their limits as has been the practice in the past, or their fate will be worse than those of dogs" (95). The revolution and counter-revolution bring the state of affairs to the brink chaos. Violence has a crucial role in the process. For centuries civilized men have been condemning 'violence as a method of change.' In the play pacifism is replaced by violence, Basavanna, is replaced by a nineteen year old firebrand 'sharana,' whose father had been a Brahmin. Bijjala is replaced by Sovideva, his treacherous and scheming son who imprisons his father and usurps his throne, and comes down heavily on the 'sharanas.' The play depicts a strong opposition and rejection of the social change, which would have improved the existing conditions but because of a handful of powerful people who reject it, they overthrow a good ruler and impose the old order which is a hydra-headed monster.

Talé-Danda is a serious work of art; it projects Karnad's socio-religious perspective. He chooses history and myth to present a represent a contemporary problem mirroring the social scenario of India today. He says in the preface to *Talé-Danda* that he thought of this play in the light of the *'Mandir'* and *'Mandal'* issue which triggered off so much of social unrest. The play shows Karnad's analysis in artistic terms of a segment of history to bring forth the unfortunate implications of its invariable repetitions in history. So many times blood has been spilt in the name of religion and caste, but to no avail. Caste bias still persists, 'sharanas' are born in every generation people like Buddha, and Gandhi, but the caste-system, religious bigotry, fanatics still exist to divide the society into factions, fanned by politicians who play the power game. The fire which is fanned by them may consume the entire country one day. This system certainly stands in the way of an all round development of the country.

Notes

Girish Karnad *Talé-Danda* (Delhi: Ravi Dayal Publishers, 1993).

Rabindranath Tagore, *Three Plays* (Madras: Oxford University Press, 1950).

USE OF MASK BY GIRISH KARNAD IN "HAYAVADAN" AND O'NEILL'S "MEMORANDA ON MASKS": RELEVANCE IN THE CONTEMPORARY CONTEXT

10

Jaya Kapoor

Girish Karnad's use of the mask technique in "Hayavadan" in reflection of O'Neill's "Memoranda on Masks" appears as an interesting study. Karnad, like O'Neill in American literature in English, is an important dramatist in the early stages of the development of the modern experimental theatre in India. And again like O'Neill, he too has learnt a lot from European theatrical traditions in the formative years.

Mask as a theatrical device is probably as old as theatre itself; and dramatists constantly turn to musing the device in their technical experiments. Even the modern drama, with all its sophisticated technical prowess still finds mask relevant to their theatrical experiments. It will be interesting to see how far the device actually works in the context of a theatre contemporary in approach and exploration.

When O'Neill started his career as a dramatist, there was an inadequate drama tradition in the experimental theatre of America which could provide creative and intellectual impetus to the mainstream theatre. The popular theatre, of which O'Neill's father was a part, was flourishing, but there was no scope for pursuit of theatrical art. O'Neill turned to European theatrical traditions for help and guidance. Schopenhauer, Nietzsche, Sartre, Thomas Mann and Freud were some of the writers who guided his talent apart from the rich traditions of Greek and English Theatre. He had to turn to European dramatic traditions to explore, expand and hone his dramatic skills. The device of mask has for long been used in the European theatre though by the Seventeenth Century it was more or less limited to use in Masques or Opera with Drama turning naturalistic and turning to the drawing room for most discussions. The use of masks is an important stage in the development of the dramatic art of O'Neill and one which kept fascinating him throughout his life. He made improvisations and changes and kept turning to masks to explore his characters at every stage of his dramatic career.

Karnad finds a special interest in the rich wealth of Indian mythology which offers him ample threads to weave his stories where he is not just narrating a tale but constructing and exploring narratives at various levels. The richest in this multilayered narrative explorations is his play "Hayavadan."

"Hayavadan" is based on a story from "Kathasaritsagar" but the idea has been taken more directly from Thomas Mann's adaptation of the tale in his "the Transposed Heads." Girish Karnad had earlier resorted to using a European format for his play based on Indian mythology in "Yayati."

The technique of masks as employed in "Hayavadan" is not to be seen in isolation with reference to the plays of Girish Karnad. He has been well versed with the dramatic structure of Western theatre and at least read, if not seen in performance dramatists including Anouilh, Sartre, O'Neill, and the Greeks. While talking about the experience of writing "Yayati" he says:

> The play owed its form not to the innumerable mythological plays I had been brought up on, and which had partly kept these myths alive for me, but to Western playwrights whom I had read only in print....[1]

The same inadequacy of dramatic tradition had been felt by O'Neill which had compelled him to turn to the European continent for thought as well as tools. Karnad uses the European format in "Hayavadan."

"Hayavadan" is the story of a woman Padmini, who marries a learned Brahmin, Devadatta, but gradually falls in love with the sensuous beauty of his best friend, Kapila. Devadatta realizes the unexpressed attraction between Padmini and Kapila, two people he loves the most in the world. Kapila too fights the attraction knowing that she is the wife of his friend and his loyalty towards his friend demands of him to keep away from her. As a result of this friction, Devadatta cuts his head off at the shrine of Goddess Kali. When Kapila discovers this he too follows his friend and cuts his head off at the altar of the Deity. Padmini discovers the tragedy and also attempts to sacrifice her head, but the Goddess stops her and grants the life of Devadatta and Kapila. Padmini by mistake, mixes the heads and torsos. As a result, Devadatta's head gets Kapila's torso while Kapila's head gets Devadatta's torso. The two men fight over who possesses Padmini now. A wise man solves the problem by giving Padmini to the body with Devadatta's head since it is held that the head is the center of being and the body is lower down in the hierarchy of limbs. Time passes and slowly the beautiful former body of Kapila begins to get back to its original shape and Padmini's ecstasy of getting the best of both the men in one body begins to wane. One day she meets Kapila in the forest and discovers that in the hard life of the forest the former body of Devadatta has become shapely like Kapila's old body. Once again Padmini is caught in the dilemma.

Kapila tells her that though his mind does not recognize the body of Padmini, his body responds to her touch intuitively and Padmini too can feel that her response to Kapila is also her response to the body of her husband. Devadatta discovers Kapila and Padmini and once again they fight for her. This time they kill each other. Padmini dies a sati on the pyre of the two men—one her husband in the body the other in the mind. And this time as well they commit a kind of suicide because what they destroyed was their own former body.

The original Sanskrit story had ended with the wise man declaring the body with Devadatta's head as the husband of Padmini, Mann expanded the story to suit his purpose. Kirtinath Kurtkoti in his introduction to the plays says:

> The original poses a moral problem while Mann uses it to ridicule the mechanical conception of life which differentiates between the body and the soul. He ridicules the philosophy which holds the head as superior to the

body. The human body, Mann argues, is a fit instrument for fulfilment of human destiny. Even the transposition of heads will not liberate the protagonist from the psychological limits imposed by nature.[2]

Thomas Mann's philosophy is closely linked to that of Schopenhauer and Freud—two people to have a deep influence on O'Neill as well. When Mann argues for the body as a fit vehicle for fulfilling destiny, what he is trying to say is that there is in every human being the head as the center of identity of the person, but the body also constitutes as a part of the system. The instincts are also a part of the system, but they are not a part of the head. The body of Devadatta responds to the touch of Padmini and try as she may, she always failed to make the body of Kapila carried by the head of Devadatta respond as the Kapila had always hesitated in his relationship with Padmini moving beyond the mind actual physical expression. Even with the face of Devadatta giving, it the freedom to respond physically to Padmini, it fails to do so. This closely resembles the romantic conception where the instinct being closer to a purely natural reaction, is considered as important as the reasoning faculty, the mind, and probably more so because it holds close affinities with the supernatural or the eternal in nature on account of being beyond the bounds of reason.

Closely resembling with this idea is the idea that O'Neill put forward in "Memoranda on Masks," while discussing a new kind of drama:

> ...a new form of drama projected from a fresh insight into the inner forces motivating the action and reactions of men and women. (A new and truer characterization in other words) ... a drama of souls, and the adventures of 'free wills,' with the masks that govern them and constitute their fates.[3]

The 'Will' acts independent of their identity and combines with the masks to direct the fate. Similarly in "Hayavadan," the exchange of heads does not change the person and the bodies respond by their own instinct. In the second part, the body of Kapila responds to Padmini as it had when it was related to Devadatta. When Padmini in spite of getting the mind of Devadatta with the body of Kapila felt uncomfortable with the body. Her dilemma is shown in her decision to die as a sati on the bodies of both Devadatta and Kapila.

Though it is granted that Karnad used mask out of the dramatic compulsions to portray the changed heads, but still the mask is a false identity put on by both the characters. If we take the mask to be merely a symbol for the face, we are making it out to be the simple moral dilemma that the original Sanskrit story was. Karnad in writing the play will certainly not be interested in it from that point of view only.

Expounding upon the difference between the approach of the West and the traditional Indian theater regarding the use of masks, Karnad points out:

> Western theater has developed a contrast between the *face* and the *mask*—the real inner person and the exterior one presents, or wishes to present, to the world outside. But in the traditional Indian theater, the mask is only the face 'writ large,' since a character represents not a complex psychological entity but an ethical archetype, the mask merely presents in enlarged detail its essential moral nature.[4]

In "Hayavadan," Karnad presents the conflict between body and the soul and by using the masks, he has in some ways brought together the Indian idea of masks as face 'writ large, and Mann's hypothesis of body as a fit vehicle for fulfilling destiny.' But in the process, he is also coming very close to the idea put forward by O'Neill in "Memoranda on Mask" as stated earlier.

Once again in "Hayavadan," Devadatta stops writing poetry. The body of Kapila that he gets is not attuned to responding to experience and so there is a discrepancy between the will and the mask that leads to the poet turning away from poetry. On the other hand, the body of Devadatta that Kapila got responds very naturally to the touch of Padmini, something that deeply disturbs Kapila as he can neither understand nor control it.

The transposed heads lead to a conflict in which the head is also an identity put on by the character. Kapila and Devadatta yearn to be each other. Kapila wishes to be Devadatta so that he can express his love to Padmini while Devadatta wishes to be Kapila so that he can charm his wife and win her love. O'Neill says in "Memoranda on Mask":

> ...the use of masked will be discovered to be the freest solution of the modern dramatist's problem as to how—with the greatest possible dramatic clarity and economy of means—he can express those hidden conflicts of the mind which the probings of Psychology continue to disclose to us.[5]

Karnad's idea behind using the mask, more than merely to portray the change of face was to depict a similar kind of conflict. "Hayavadan" begins not with the story of Padmini but with the incident of the horse-bodied boy which gives the play its name. Here the horse is a symbol of conflict that is produced by the identity that is not a natural part of the being but put on from outside and at the end of the play the creature loses even the human face and becomes a horse altogether leading to a resolution of the conflict. The plot is built in the style of story within a story. Both the story of the horse bodied boy and that of the lovers explore the same theme of an adopted identity growing into the actual identity.

But in case of Kapila and Devadatta their conflicts of identity cannot be so simply resolved and the end as their death is the only feasible solution to the situation. There is no other way in which they could have accepted a resolution of their crisis. Going back to their old bodies could only have made the situation more complex. The idea is to present the conflict as a result of putting on a false identity that a reversal would not have brought on as effectively.

O'Neill comments in "Memoranda on Mask":

> ...what, at the bottom is the new psychological insight into human cause and effect but a study in masks, an exercise in unmasking? ...this insight has uncovered the mask, has impressed the idea of mask as a symbol of inner reality upon all intelligent people of today; and I know they would welcome the use of mask in the theater as a

necessary, dramatically revealing new convention, and not regard them as any 'stunty' resurrection of archaic props.[6]

Karnad's experiments with mask echoes similar ideas although he points out to the difference between the western and the Indian concept of the masks, as mentioned earlier but still he has learned from the Western experimental theater and his approach in "Hayavadan" reflects this influence. In the light of the above statement of O'Neill, it can be seen that though "Memoranda on Mask" is not directly related to "Hayavadan" but the idea of mask as a false identity comes very close to the play and helps in coming to a better understanding of the mask as used in the play.

"Memoranda on Mask" reflects the understanding process in O'Neill regarding those aspects of human nature that lie behind the visible persona. It also helps in tracing that which has remained essentially human despite the developments that mark culture and civilization. The mythology provides a rich metaphor for such sustaining human qualities and mask reveals those qualities in the backdrop of day-to-day life.

Karnad's plays too have developed from the use of mask as a device to reveal the inner traits through subtler replacements of the mask. The continuing relevance of mythology for both these dramatists even at later stages of their dramatic career leads us to ponder over the significance of mythology for enunciating what is essentially human through all the ages and changes. And more importantly mask merges as a tool for exploring these qualities in case of both the play writers and an important place in their development as playwrights.

References

1. Girish Karnad, *Three Plays.* New Delhi: Oxford University Press, 2000, 3.
2. "Hayavadan," New Drama in India. New Delhi: O.U.P., 1998, v.
3. The Unknown O'Neill, ed. Trains Bogard, New Haven, Yale University, 1998, 406.
4. Girish Karnad, *Three Plays.* New Delhi: Oxford University Press, 2003, 3.
5. The Unknown O'Neill, Trains. Bogard, New Haven, Yale University, 1988, 406.
6. *Ibid.*, 406.

SOCIAL ALIENATION IN KARNAD'S *TUGHLAQ*

11

Priya Srivastava

Girish Karnad known as India's leading living playwright, the most prominent and renowned media personality, a writer of native tradition, is at his best as a dramatist. A gifted actor, he acts in both Kannada and Hindi Commercial films; Produces and directs off beat Kannada and Hindi films (*Sanskara* in Kannada, *Utsav* in Hindi) and also popular serials for Doordarshan. He defends freedom of expression and entertainment in films with equal vehemence. Karnad's contribution to art, culture, theatre and drama has brought him immense popularity and has enriched the Indian literary scene. His plays either mythical, historical or legendry have received an international recognition. Though modern his plays uphold the traditional values also. Karnad, a bilingual writer writes his plays first in Kannada and then renders them into English which qualify to be a part of Indian-English drama. His English versions of Kannada plays are better than the originals. He sought into prominence with the publication of his plays. *Tughlaq,*[1] which is Karnad's second Kannada play and now widely recognized as a classic, first appeared in 1964 and was a great success on the stage. This play alone has established Karnad as a noted dramatist. Although the theme of the play is from history—there are many such plays in Kannada where Karnad's treatment of the theme is not historical. It throws light on the life, nature and psyche of a medieval monarch Sultan Mohammad Tughlaq, whose reign is considered to be one of the spectacular regimes of History. Being a sensitive and intelligent ruler who sets out to do the best for his people, Tughlaq was misunderstood and maligned, suffers an increasing sense of alienation and is forced to abandon his earlier idealism and end up as a tyrant. Karnad delved deep into the legend and made it a vehicle of a new vision. He tried to show the absurdity of life with all its elemental passions and conflicts and man's eternal struggle to achieve perfection. Thus the play deals with the theme of alienation with existential overtones.

Karnad's Tughlaq has been compared by critics to Camu's Caligula and Eisentein's Ivan the terrible, where in the play he is seen as a deracinated monarch whose absolute individualism alienated him from his people, from society and from himself. He emphasises on the personal reality of individual existence and so as a man he is doomed to suffer the corrosive impact of alienation. Edmund fuller views, "man suffers not only from war, persecution, famine and ruin, but from inner problems...a conviction of isolation, randomness, (and) meaninglessness in his way of existence."[2] The pervasive sense of alienation has corroded human life from various quarters and the man has shrunk in spirit languishing in confusion, frustration, disintegration, disillusionment and alienation.

The concept of alienation is not quiet new and it has been in vogue in philosophical, theological, sociological and psychological writings for a long time. The sufferings from an acute sense of rootlessness, which may manifest itself as "the alienation from oneself, from one's fellow men and from nature; the awareness that life runs out of one's hand like sand...."[3] It is seen that there is always a struggle between what the individual aspires for and the harsh reality of what he achieves, what he professes and what he practises, what he really is and what he would like to be taken for, has crumpled his life leaving an insidious effect on his inner being. The injuries inflicted and the scars left on his psyche make him realise only of his helplessness. Painfully aware of his precarious position, man experiences severe limitations arising out of randomness and alienation.

The plight of an individual as discussed by Melvin Seaman in five interrelated operational conditions, *viz.*, powerlessness, meaningless, normlessness, isolation and self-estrangement which are nothing but different manifestations of alienation. The most obvious repercussion of alienation can be seen in a person's fractured consciousness and his "fractionated functions."[4] There can be several layers and kinds of alienation. Taviss mentions two different kinds of alienation, *i.e.* "Social alienation" and "Self-alienation." Social alienation results from the sense of estrangement brought out by the sudden discovery, that the social system is either oppressive or incomplete or incompatible with their desires and ideals. Self-alienation, however, means the loss of contact of the individual selves with any inclinations or desires that are not in agreement with the prevailing social patterns as a results of which the individuals are forced to manipulate in accordance with the social demands or feel incapable of controlling their actions.[5] To be socially alienated thus means man's dehumanization, his loss of freedom and his estrangement from other human beings. Man is an alienated outsider figure, estranged at various levels from the individuals around him and the society, from existence of self and the human predicament in this world. Broadly speaking, man's social-alienation implies his estrangement from his family, his community, his society and eventually from his own self. He is estranged from the society because he is a man ahead of his age and is not understood by the society around him because his ideals and ideals are far above and very different from an ordinary human being. Man upholds that he can transcend reality in his own consciousness and can assert for himself despite his limitations and failures. This results in the social alienation of the protagonist from traditions, society and from individuals around him.

Karnad's *Tughlaq*, is the first in "New Drama in India"—a series which is outstanding in contemporary Indian plays. This play explores the paradox of the idealistic king Tughlaq who does not have a single moment of peace and rest, as he is always suspicious of the motives of the people close to him. The number of imposters, betrayers, rebels and treacherous people around him never lent him any real support. The people thought him mad and the Amirs termed him tyrannical. He, a formidable ruler who would not let anybody or anything come in his way of power and the answer to his resistance is his sword. Tughlaq is an usurper having come to the throne after getting his father and brother murdered during prayer time, having committed heinous crimes and his unpopular schemes created many foes for him, and the transformation of the character of the ruler from a sensitive and intelligent ruler who sets out to do his best for his people ends up into pieces. This was due to both his idealism as well as his shortcomings within him which led him to further alienation.

From the opening scene this play unfolds the dreams and aspirations of an overambitious, yet virtuous king of Delhi—Mohammad Bin-Tughlaq. He, from the very beginning, is traced as a man who is estranged from the society around him because of his different ideas. He has been denounced by the historians as a mad king. It is seen that he was a ruler in search of human beings, not Hindus or Muslims. In this scene the ruler is highlighted as a secular king in a true sense who never differentiated between caste or creed and granted a Hindu "the said Vishnu Prasad a post in the civil service to ensure him a regular and adequate income" (3). He tries to show justice to his people without any partiality for any particular community but his broadmindedness seems foolish to the Muslims and cunning to the Hindus who suspect his motives.

Tughlaq's plans regarding the change of capital of his empire from Delhi to Daulatabad sounds reasonable but fails to convince his people and his subjects largely criticize him. This startling announcement,

> Muhammad: Later this year the capital of my empire will be moved from Delhi to Daulatabad.... Your surprise is natural, but I beg you to realize that this is no mad whim of a tyrant...." (3)

His views regarding the change is that he wants to see his kingdom flourish and prosper. Daulatabad is a city of Hindus and this symbolizes the bond between the two religions *i.e.* Hindus and Muslims and he wishes to develop and strengthen in his kingdom. Tughlaq tries to justify his step of shifting the capital. He says, "My Empire is large now and embraces the south and I need a capital which is at its heart. Delhi is too near the border" (3). But the play shows the tragic consequences of the life of the visionary ruler who was not able to make his dreams come true and he meets with stiff opposition from all classes of people.

Scene two presents the frustration of Sultan at the non-comprehension of his plans regarding the change of capital. "But how can I spread my branches in the stars while the roots have yet to find their hold in the earth?" (10). Despite of all his efforts to win the confidence of his subjects and build an ideal empire he fully realized the tragedy of his predicament as all his efforts finally failed and his idealistic dreams can never reach the stars unless they are rooted in the firm support of his people. He is not understood by the society around him and so the social alienation of Tughlaq from his people were finally responsible for the failure of his schemes. Tughlaq is also alienated at the interpersonal level from the individuals around him. His interpersonal alienation is firstly, seen in manipulating people for his own purposes, treating them as objects and not persons, and secondly, he is also unable to establish meaningful communication with others and is seen to be play-acting continually. Tughlaq indulges in role-play not only in public but this is also seen in his private conversation with his step-mother where it seems that he is acting when she asks him why he does not sleep at night he becomes theatrical in answering her and she bursts into laughter with the amused comment,

> Step-Mother: (bursts into laughter): "I can't ask a simple question without your giving a royal performance" (10-11). According to Erving Gaffman, "To the degree that the individual maintains a show before others...he can come to experience a special kind of alienation from self."[6]

Third scene presents Tughlaq, as alienated in his relationship with men who see each other not as human beings but as objects which can be used to achieve their own goals. Taghlaq is seen as a clever manipulator who arranges a prayer meeting in honour of Sheikh Imam-ud-din which is actually a trap laid cleverly by the Sultan who wants to get rid of him and Ain-ul-Mulk at one stroke. The Sultan persuades the Imam to go as his envoy and dissuade Ain-ul-Mulk of Avadh who is marching on Delhi at that very moment. The Imam accepts this request, although he does not trust the motives of the king and feels that he is left with no other alternative. Tughlaq sees others through an alienated vision—not as persons but as pawns, objects to be used and discarded. "Why should the Sultan sponsor his worst critic? They have smelt a trap. And wisely they have stayed away" (22). Thus he gets rid of his greatest critic and get indulges in seemingly genuine grief for the Sheikh.

Scenes four and five discuss Tughlaq's desire for an ideal empire but fails to carry his people along with him. The people take him as a man of distrust and therefore they do not like his proposal of shifting his capital. One of the Amirs tell,

> Amir I: Why is he taking us from Delhi to Daulatabad? Have you even thought over this matter? Is it not surprising? I tell you his plan is to weaken the Amirs. You see we are strong in Delhi. This is where we belong. But Daulatabad is a Hindu city and we'll be helpless there. We'll have to lick his feet." (31)

His crafty nature is exposed to the people and his ideals and policies are vigorously resisted and challenged and so he fails to convince his subjects and feels frustrated at their non-comprehension.

Tughlaq, as is seen that despite of all his efforts he is not able to win the confidence of his people around him and he fully realizes the tragedy of his predicament which is visible in scene six,

> Muhammad: But how can I explain tomorrow to those who haven't even opened their eyes to the light of today? (39)

Tughlaq's alienation from his people is responsible for the failure of his schemes. He feels that if people fail to understand his schemes then he too fails to foresee their reactions. He not only proposes a change of capital involving at the administrative level but also of the people, lock, stock and barrel and overlooking the emotional attachment of the people to their native soil,

> Shihab-ud-Din: "I implore your majesty not to move the capital. But I know the people of Delhi are unhappy about the move. (39)

He did not also foresee and take precautions against the possibility of counterfeiting when he proposes to introduce copper currency along with the silver dinars,

> Muhammad: "From next year we have copper currency in our empire along with the silver dinars." (39)

People do not trust his plans and take him as a mad Sultan though he tries to convince his people, his repeated failure in missing the confidence of the public paves the way for his gradual disillusionment and fall from his ideals which ultimately leads him to a further alienation from society.

In Tughlaq's relationship with others there is very little genuine communication. He distances from others by adopting a role, which becomes a matter of anguish for him. Alienated from the society and the individuals around him in scene eight it is seen that Tughlaq is passing through a crisis. His policies have failed. His idealistic illusions are shattered. The shifting of the capital from Delhi to Daulatabad has been a painful experience for everybody his subjects even call him "Mad Muhammad"[7] and the Sultan wants to become wise again. But he also cannot admit that he has been wrong all those years, for he still feels that he has something to give to his subjects though he becomes a tyrant. In the same scene at the end we see Tughlaq's present degeneration in Barani's appeal to Tughlaq:

> Barani: "Your majesty, there was a time when you believed in love, is peace in God, what has happened to those ideals?.... why this bloodshed? Please stop it." (56)

Barani suggests Tughlaq that he should review his relationship with God and neighbour. Tughlaq is not prepared to do so for it would mean that he had been wrong all those years. He does not admit to this and feels he has a mission to accomplish, a lesson to teach. If people respond only to cruelty and violence, then he will use only those means to reach his end.

In the play, the series of events which results in Tughlaq's progressive alienation from society make him realize the vast gulf between ideals and reality, aspirations and fulfilment. In scene ten, the Sultan realizes that his innovative measures taken from time to time for the benefit of his subjects *i.e.* change of capital and introduction of copper currency proved fatal. The rose garden which was visible as a symbol of visionary hopes to create a Utopia, becomes a rubbish dump where fake copper coins are piled up. He says,

> Muhammad: "Now I don't need a rose garden. I built it because I wanted for myself...I wanted every rose in it to be a poem.... But I don't need those airy trappings now. A funeral has no need for a separate symbol." (63-64)

His past idealism with the present corruption is also traced in this scene when his stepmother tells Tughlaq, that his glorious empire which was at one time idealistic and full of hopes has now become a kitchen of death,

> Step-mother: "Look at your kingdom now. It's become a kitchen of death." (65)

But Tughlaq is ready to confess that violence is no longer under his control and therefore adopted tyranny as a way of life, a vehicle to fulfil his mission in life. It is visible that Tughlaq experiences intense self-estrangement after condemning his stepmother to death in this scene. Left alone he desperately pleads with God to help him,

> Muhammad: "God, God in Heaven, please help me please don't let go of my hand...I started in your path, lord, why am I wandering naked in this desert now?" (67)

In this tone of despair and helplessness he realizes that his own strength is not enough to sustain him and so he needs to pray. He realizes his own self-alienation and knows that he has reached the extreme edge of self-estrangement, which is madness.

Tughlaq again indulges in play-acting and self-dramatization in scene eleven. He dramatically falls at the feet of Aziz Ghiyas-ud-din.

> Muhammad: "Welcome to our city, your holiness, welcome to our poor land. My kingdom rejoices at the arrival of your gracious presence." (71)

This histrionic gesture has its effect on the crowd but they express their discontentment because they are in need of food and not prayers. The Sultan is not able to understand their plight though he tries to bring comfort to his people but his steps are untimely. Scene twelve expresses Tughlaq's anguish at the trick played on him by life—it had promised him a rose garden and gave him a rubbish dump. He wanted to rule a Utopia but ended up ruling a Kitchen of death. This contrast between man's expectations and the harsh realities pushes him into alienation from self as well as the society.

Tughlaq reaches a dead end in complete exhaustion by the end of the play as Barani also passes out of his life. He is left completely exhausted and he falls asleep just, as prayer is restored in his kingdom after a ban of five years. The sleep is a symbol of the failures of Sultan who realizes that all his ideal steps have come to naught. His friends have either died or they have proved to be treacherous. Characters like Najib, Barani, Azam and Aziz highlight certain elements of alienation. The game of chess and the rose garden are two important images and serves as metaphors of alienation and may be related to Tughlaq's alienation. Chess symbolizes Tughlaq's game approach to life and the rose garden transformed into a rubbish dump is perfectly related with Tughlaq's defeat, frustration and disillusionment in his life. He is projected as a highest frustrated man where his men are discontented and he is not able to contemplate his real position in the present critical circumstances.

Thus, Karnad in his play presents Tughlaq as an alienated personality who experiences social and interpersonal alienation and self-estrangement. The other characters are also seen where they experience alienation, which serves to highlight Tughlaq's predicament. He is alienated from the society in which he lives and in his quest to prove his superiority he forgets that he himself is a living being. He wants to be different from other and in this he dehumanizes himself and intensifies his alienation.

Notes

1. Girish Karnad, *Tughlaq* in *Three Modern Indian Plays* (Delhi: Oxford U.P., 1989).
2. *Man in Modern Fiction* (New York, 1958), 3.
3. Erich Fromm et al., *Zen Buddhism and Psychoanalysis* (New York, 1970), 86.
4. Frank Johnson (ed.), *Alienation: Concept, Term and Meaning* (New York and London, 1973), 46.
5. I. Taviss, "Changes in the Form of Alienations," *American Sociological Review*, 34/1 (February 1969), 46-47.
6. Erving Goffmann, *The Presentation of Self in Everyday Life* (New York: Doubleday Anchor, 1959), 236.
7. Span number, 36 Postcolonial Fictions: R.P. Rama "Once upon a time there was an Emperor": A Reading of *Tughlaq*, a Modern Indian play by Girish Karnad, 2.

HISTORICAL PERSPECTIVE IN KARNAD'S *TUGHLAQ*

12

R.P. Pradhan

Tughlaq is the best historical play of Girish Karnad. It is a notable contribution to the development of Indo-Anglian drama. The dramatist has taken up the last five years of the reign of Sultan Muhammad Tughlaq who ascended the throne of Delhi in 1325 A.D. and ruled India till his death in 1351. Other historical events of the time of the Sultan have been reported through the conversations of various characters. Hence the play offers a comprehensive study of the period under review.

Karnad tries to maintain fidelity to history and presents the historical events and complexities of the time in an objective manner. However, keeping in view the artistic necessity he deviates from history here and there and throws upon the events a beautiful colouring of art and imagination. The dramatist introduces a few changes in the historical lines because he intends to make the play relevant to contemporary situations of the sixties when the country was passing through a phase of disillusionment after the death of Pt. Nehru. The dramatist himself writes that what struck him most about Tughlaq's history was that it was contemporary. He found that there was the most idealistic, the most intelligent king who ever came to the throne of Delhi. The king had met the greatest faiiure in the annals of Indian history Karnad writes:

> And within a span of twenty years this tremendously capable man had gone to pieces. This seemed to be both due to his impatience, his cruelty, his feeling that he had the only correct answer. And I felt in the early sixties that India had also come very far in the same direction—the twenty years period seemed to me very much a striking parallel.[1]

Karnad has presented Tughlaq as a bundle of contradictions and a queer mixture of the opposites. The complex personality of Sultan at once made him a dreamer and also a man of action, a benevolent ruler and a malevolent politician, a god-like and a godless figure. Most of his plans were Utopian, fantastic and visionary. They ended in fiasco and brought about untold human suffering on a large scale. However they always appeared to be the product of his original and fertile brain. His reign is considered to be one of the most spectacular failures in the Indian history but it is also admitted by a few eminent historians that the Sultan was unquestionably the ablest man among the Indian rulers of the middle age.

Karnad sticks to history in presenting Tughlaq as a just and generous king. In the opening scene the Sultan appears as a deeply religious person. He has no partiality for any particular community and makes an attempt for Hindu-Muslim unity. For him all are equal in the eyes of law and hence he announces that the property of Vishnu Prasad must be restored. Vishnu Prasad is, a Brahmin of Shinkar whose land has been seized illegally by the officers of the State. The Sultan further sanctions him a grant of five hundred silver dinars and a post in civil service. The incident refers to his sense of justice, generosity and fair play in his kingdom.

In the opening scene Tughlaq also declares his intention of shifting his capital from Delhi to Daulatabad. The dramatist points to its disastrous consequences on the common people and they are corroborated by history as well. Karnad's *Tughlaq* justifies the change of capital by saying that his empire is large and embraces the south. He needs a capital in the heart of the empire. Delhi is near the border and its peace is disturbed by the invaders. Besides, Daulatabad is a city of Hindus and the change shall symbolize the bond between Muslims and Hindus which the king wishes to develop and strengthen in his kingdom. Girish Karnad presents the act of shifting of the capital as only the product of the whim of the Sultan. He brings into light the failures and the weaknesses of the king. His views are based mostly on the opinions of Barani and not on other historians. According to Barani Tughlaq played with the lives of the people in his kingdom. He was whimsical and despotic ruler. He made plans out of his whims and forced his people to follow them. If they failed to do so they were severely punished.

Historical Tughlaq is said to be guilty of patricide and fratricide. The dramatist refers to it in the play through the statement of the third man in the first scene that he has heard that the Sultan is guilty of killing his father and brother. History also tells about the feeling of remorse and repentance which Tughlaq observed over the murder of his father but Karnad does not mention any such feelings in the heart of Tughlaq. The humanism and idealism of Tughlaq referred to in history has found expression also in the play. In scene second Tughlaq talks about his visions to his stepmother that they should pray till their bodies melt and flow and their blood turns into air, they should pray to become light and cover the earth with greenery:

> I pray to Almighty to save me from sleep. All day long I have to worry about tomorrow but it is only when the night falls that I can step beyond all that.[2]

The dramatist seems to point out that sheer idealism in lack of the spirit of realism is bound to meet crisis and failure in the end whether in the fourteenth or in the twentieth century.

According to the historians Tughlaq was a great lover of learning in general and of Greek learning in particular. In the play, Tughlaq expresses his inclination towards the great philosophers:

> I still remember the days when I read the Greeks—Sukrat who took poison so he could give the world the drink of gods. Aflatoon who condemned poets and wrote incomparably beautiful poetry himself—and I can still feel the thrill with which I found a new world, a world I had not found in the Arabs or even the Koran. You are asking me to make myself complete by killing the Greek in me and you propose to unify my people by denying the visions which led Zarathustra or the Buddha.[3]

The introduction of token currency was the most significant innovation of Tughlaq in the history of India. In the sixth scene of the play the Sultan informs that from next year his people shall have copper currency in their empire along with silver dinars and a copper coin will have the same value as a silver coin. In the eighth scene the Sultan cannot sleep because his people make counterfeit copper coins. They even call him "Mad Muhammad" and Sultan wants to become wise again. In scene ten the Sultan realizes that if he does not withdraw copper coins, the whole economy of his kingdom shall be shattered. Girish Karnad portrays this event only to show the utter failure of Tughlaq. Historians say that introduction of copper currency was not a strange step of Tughlaq. Such currency had been successful in China and Iran also. Tughlaq took this step on account of the shortage of silver. The attitude of the dramatist is not sympathetic in this matter.

In history Najib is not an important character as he is in the play. The dramatist shows him as the evil genius of Tughlaq. On account of it Najib is got murdered by the stepmother. In the same way the episode of Aziz and Aazam has also been introduced by Karnad in order to provide dramatic relief. It projects also the administrative failure of Tughlaq. The comic episode occurs in scene nine in which Aziz speaks to Aazam:

> If you remain virtuous throughout your life no one will say a good thing about you because they won't need to. But start stealing—and they will say: "What a nice boy he was. But he is ruined now."[4]

This comic remark is allegorical and makes an indirect comment on the fall of the Sultan.

In the eleventh scene we are led to a plain outside the fort of Daulatabad, where there is a big crowd of dejected people. They do not want prayer, they want food. In the thirteenth scene the famine riots, have already spread on a wide scale. Daulatabad is in shambles. Even Barani, the writer, wants to leave the place. Such scenes echo historical events of the age and throw light on the sad and pitiful conditions of the people in the empire.

Tughlaq is not an ordinary chronicle play but it is an imaginative reconstruction of history in the modern context.

In the play history is mixed with politics and the dramatist seems to show that politics is used to promote the self-interest of the leaders and not the welfare of the people. In scene VII Aziz, the disguised washerman, says:

> My dear fellow, that is where our future is—politics! It is a beautiful world—wealth, success, position, power—and it is full of brainless people, people with not an idea in their head.[5]

The dramatist also portrays through the scenes of the play that politics is mixed with religion and religion is made use of by the politicians for their selfish motives. The character of the Sultan is full of dualism. As a faithful Muslim he prescribes prayer five times a day but he kills his father and brother while they are at prayer. The revered Sheikh Imam is doing the job of an envoy. The Sultan has managed to kill him in such a way that nobody might doubt it.

Several readers and spectators of the play likened it to the Nehru era in Indian history but Karnad did not support it. To him such similarity might be accidental. He says:

> I did not consciously write about the Nehru era. I am always flattered when people tell me that it was about the Nehru era and equally applies to the development of politics since then. But, I think well, that is a compliment that any playwright would be thrilled to get but it was not intended to be a contemporary play about a contemporary situation.[6]

However the note of symbolism and allegory seems to be employed to make this historical play relevant to the modern conditions of India.

Notes

1. Paul, Rajendra, Girish Karnad Interviewed Enact No. 54, June 1986. Sarup and Sons, 35.
2. Girish Karnad, *Tughlaq* (Delhi: Oxford University Press, 1972), 26.
3. *Ibid.*, 21.
4. *Ibid.*, 57.
5. *Ibid.*, 50.
6. Paul, Rajendra, Girish Karnad Interviewed: Enact No. 54, June 1986. Sarup and Sons, 35.

MAHESH DATTANI AND BADAL SIRCAR

MAHESH DATTANI AND BADAL SIRCAR

13

Neeru Tandon

MAHESH DATTANI

Born a leo on August 7, 1958, in Bangalore, Mahesh Dattani is a graduate in History, Economics and Political Science. He is a post-graduate in Marketing and Advertising Management. He has been described as one of India's best and most serious contemporary playwrights writing in English by Alexandra views in the *International Herald Tribune*. Mahesh Dattani is India's first playwright in English to be awarded the Sahitya Akademi Award for his contribution to world drama. His plays deal with religious tension, sexuality and gender issues. What one loves about them is the way he brings in the dynamics of personal and moral choices while focusing on human relationships. Theatre director Alyque Padamsree calls him one of the 'most serious contemporary playwrights.' And what's more, he is a director actor dancer, teacher and writer all rolled into one. As actor he has starred in several well-known plays and has won accolades for his sterling performance in them. They include *A Macbeth* (1987), *Where There's a Will* (1988), *Dance Like a Man* (1989), *The Tempest* (1995), *Henry IV* (2001).

Dattani has held senior positions in theatre groups and institutions. In 1987 he was chosen as Artistic Director, founder of PLAYPEN performing arts group, Bangalore. In 1994 he worked as Senior Associate, National Institute for Advanced Studies, Bangalore. In 1988 he established 'Mahesh's Studio—a Centre for the performing arts.' In 1999 he was appointed as Senior Trustee, Swabhava—a charitable trust.

In 2000, he appeared as Trustee of VOICES, a development organisation supported by Ford Foundation. Dattani's dedication and passion for theatre has won him scholarships and awards, besides being commissioned by top national and international bodies to write plays on social issues for them. His awards include: Sahitya Kala Parishad for best production of *Dance Like a Man* (1997), *Bravely Fought the Queen* (1998), Sahitya Akademi Award, in 1988 for book of plays Final Solutions and other plays, in 2000; Sahitya Kala Parishad award for best production of 'Tara.'

Mahesh Dattani is a visiting professor at the Portland State University in the U.S. He has been conducting classes and workshops at the university on a regular basis, besides being a participant at the PIP fest. In 2000, he took weekend classes on Dramatic structure at Haystack, Canon Beach, Origon, USA.

His favourite playwrights would include Tennessee Williams, and in India, Vijay Tendulkar. He has now got a theatre studio in South Bangalore. As he considers that his milieu is theatre and he do wanted a theatre movement to happen. He says "The major block for that is lack of sound training and professionalism." We have the talent, but theatre is more than that: It's a craft of communicating through the language of action. I'm also working on another film project "Ek Alag Mausam" film based on Dattani's film script, is ready for release which is under wraps. Mahesh Dattani, the only Indian asked to write a talk for Chaucer's 600th anniversary. Mahesh Dattani is an internationally acclaimed playwright. After getting Akademi Award in 1988 for his play 'Final Solutions,' a gripping play on communalism, he has become the first Indian-English dramatist to receive such award. His writing credits include:

Plays

1988 – Where There's a Will

1989 – Dance Like a Man

1990 – Tara

1991 – Bravely Fought the Queen

1992-93	–	Final Solutions
1996	–	Night Queen (Short Play)
1997	–	Do The Needful (Radio play for BBC)
1998	–	On A Muggy Night in Mumbai, Seven Circles Round The Fire (Radio play for BBC)
2000	–	The Swami and Winston (Radio play for BBC)
2001	–	Thirty days in September.

Screenplay

1992	–	Chalo Memsahib (Co-wrote for Shunyata films, directed by Ayesha Sayani)
1994	–	Hum, Tum Aur Who (for Tutu films)
1996	–	Untitled Script for Govind Nihlani
2000	–	A Walk with Mr. William

International projects

2001	-	Spice Boy

Mahesh does take time off his hectic schedule to conduct workshops for the sake of maturing new talent and giving a new dimension to theatre. Mahesh has been involved in various other projects also. His awards include: Sahitya Kala Parishad for best production of *Dance Like a Man* (1997), *Bravely Fought the Queen*, Sahitya Akademi Award (1988), Sahitya Kala Parishad Award for *Tara* (2000), Mario Relich, Wasafiri, "A playwright of world stature."

"Mr. Dattani is a canny and facile writer, and there is nothing (in his writing) that is alien to American audiences, Powerful and disturbing"—Stephen Bruckner, *The New York Times*.

"Since Salman Rushdie swung open the door to the West, English Language Indian novelists have moved the world. Indian playwrights have been less conspicuous except for Mahesh Dattani"—Vibhuti Patel, *Newsweek International*.

BADAL SIRCAR

Badal Sircar a great Bengali playwright, is among the three great contemporary writers—Karnad, Vijay Tendulkar and Mohan Rakesh. Badal Sircar delves deep into the problems of middle-class society. He uses contemporary situations to project the existential attitude of modern life. Popularly known as a 'barefoot playwright' Badal Sircar stands in the forefront of a new theatrical movement in India. He has created a genuine people's theatre known as Third Theatre, a theatre supported and created by the People, and not merely performed by the people. His later plays, *Procession*, *Bhoma* and *State News*, are based on the concept of the Third Theatre. Badal Sircar's professional career as an urban planner, his training as a civil engineer is mixed with his inner life as a playwright and its outward expression in his role as a theatre director and actor. More than writing Sircar prefers doing theatre. This he wants to accomplish by what he said "trekking to the villages and rural areas in the near future."

"If there is any play-wright in the contemporary Bengali theatre who is capable of creating a genuine people's theatre a theatre supported and created by the people and not merely performed by the people, it is Badal Sircar."—*Veena Noble Dass*

(*Contemporary Indian Drama*, edited by Sudhakar Pandey and Preya Taraporewala, New Delhi: Prestige Books, 1990) 69.

Sircar started his dramatic career with some comedies and came to the lime light in 1965 with his celebrated Evam Indrajit.

AUDIENCE PARTICIPATION IN STREET PLAYS

14

Nita Jain

"Playgoing is an art," wrote J.L. Styan, in his *Elements of Drama*. "Both skill and a certain amount of discipline are required to enjoy a play. A play can be judged by the value of those who watch it."[1] Audience participation is an important concept, which can be gauged from the force in the nature of a play.

The play began as an instrument of public expression, where roaming minstrels picked up ideas close to the heart of the masses, clothed them in the language of the masses and presented action that held them spell-bound. As drama flourished, dramatic technique became an important preoccupation that brought about a distancing of drama from the 'watching' public...perhaps the actors got too much under the skin of the characters or did not consider the feelings or the emotions of the audience at all. A theory of 'alienation' or 'estrangement' developed and according to Bertolt Brecht it was done to induce "an inquiring, critical attitude on the part of the spectators towards the events shown."[2]

However there have been some interesting experiments in the present century to "reclaim this intimacy"[3] of the spectator with the actor and so today more than ever before this concept of "Audience participation" has become an alluring and an interesting concept. A critical attitude on the part of the spectator is developed, as the actor does not identify with the character he represents, rather he could chose from any particular point of view regarding the character...give his own opinion of the character or even invite the audience to criticize the character he represents. In such situations scenery is supplied by suggestion and the audience is surreptitiously drawn into the action. This drama makes for exciting participation.

Street Plays or the Indian "Nukkad Natak," today are an important contribution towards mobilization of public opinion and are being put to excellent social, political, economic and cultural reformatory and educational uses. Street Plays have become great weapons in the hands of theatre people. They are also referred to as "Fringe Theatre."[4] In America they call the street play—"Happening." The classical plays of Shakespeare or Kalidas cannot be performed on the street. The street play has to be written keeping in mind the mood of the passers by. As a matter of fact it is an ideal weapon to arouse social and political consciousness. Popular media like cinema and cable TV is entertainment media, which by and large, produces a decadent and a reactionary culture. Street theatre promotes a democratic, secular, and rational consciousness among the people while at the same time providing robust entertainment without any cost. It is very close to reality. It is focused on its aim...that it serves a social cause. Street theatre aims at sensitizing masses to social issues, enrolling them in the process of a social change and ultimately helps in the promotion of peace and harmony. It does not necessarily provide answers to the issues raised, but tries to analyze the problems. It could use humour, to satirize problems and issues. Unlike theatre in the proscenium, street theatre entails minimum use of lights, cosmetics, costumes and other techniques. "A character is established with a small but significant item of property,"[5] *e.g.*, a stick to portray a policeman, which can even be used as a prop for a flute, etc., a stool or a chair would be used to signify a king's throne etc. The actor communicates with varying tones of his voice, his body language while maintaining "eye-to-eye" contact with the audience. Episodic in structure, using choric dialogues quite often, street theatre combines music, song and dance. Street theatre makes it possible to reach people where theatre is not accessible to the majority like the streets, markets, slums, villages, schools, office complexes, parks, residential areas. It is a sort of "free show" for every one, whether he is a shopkeeper, an officer, a labourer, a housewife or a student. Then again the street play does not have constraints of a limited or a repeat audience. People from all walks of life, from different strata of society are put on the same platform...in a way it succeeds in shunning hierarchy. Dialogues and action begin to flow as they get to be delivered almost extempore.

The history of street theatre dates back to the 19th century when labourers and party workers wrote and performed plays during the Industrial Revolution in Europe. Women too participated actively and freely in plays during the suffragette movement in London at the beginning of the twentieth century. The Russian Revolution also generated among the sensitive an attempt to reach out to the illiterate and the unaware sufferers in remote areas. During World War II, the street theatre played a crucial role in tempering public opinion. Plays in America and England addressed issues related to the students' movements, women related movements, racial discrimination and the Vietnam War. There is a history of street theatre in India too where folk artists have successfully created "street magic." With the passage of time themes changed from national consciousness to capitalism, peasant and labour movements, environmental issues, communalism, dowry, the girl-child sexual harassment issues, AIDS, globalization issues, etc., etc., etc. There is the Street Theatre we commonly associate with Covent Garden that also has its antecedents in earlier history. The audience participation that one sees in the piazza including the balancing acts and chairs, (http://www.covent-garden.co.uk/historieso/swordeaters.html) is a reflection from theatrical activity in ancient Egypt and Greece.

"The sensational aspect of street theatre can be seen in a series of dangerous tricks bordering on magic including fire-throwing, eating and sword swallowing, (http://www.covent-garden.co.uk/historieso/swordeaters.html) not to mention walking on high wires." Audiences are invited to experience the work of seasoned veterans alongside that of emerging artists. You could meet them in the most unexpected places—

behind the vegetable complex in your market place, during your evening walk, at the bus stop or perhaps even on the street in front of your office—a group of people, acting out a short skit or play, for any one who might wish to stop and watch. They are not just philanthropists providing free entertainment. For them this is a means of reaching people of all strata and creating an awareness of events around them, calling them to change what they believe are the social ailments. These are the street theatre 'activists.' Street theatre is a situation where the audience has not come prepared to watch a play, and people may not have much time on hand. These limitations determine the parameters of the plays. They are short. The exchange is close, direct and intimate and, to be more effective, usually loud and larger than life. The script and direction is always significant. In order to draw crowds from all walks of life, the plays are humorous. Songs based on popular catchy tunes are included to add to its appeal. The choreography of the play varies from script to script. The play must be as inexpensive and mobile as possible, since no stage props can be used. Street theatre actors are mainly teachers and students committed to bringing about social change. Their returns in terms of finances or fame are nil. The time that this form of theatre demands is considerable. All evenings and weekends are spent rehearsing or preparing for the performance. The play is a joint effort. Each member has to agree completely on the theme for a production to go through. The script is usually written jointly as the play progresses. Of course different groups have varying aims. The Jana Natya Manch in Delhi for example performs plays on current topics. This demands that the play be produced as soon as possible to be relevant. In India Badal Sircar, the late Safdar Hashmi, Habib Tanvir and Utpal Dutt have used street theatre as political and social weapons. Nukkad Natak was revived in the 1970s and now they are popular all over the country. There are about 50 groups in the country, mainly in cities and their immediate suburbs.

Performing in the street, outdoors or on makeshift staging anywhere is not as easy as it looks. The performer needs to recognize that certain aspects of the performance must be enhanced if the piece is to work as intended. Most amateur actors fail to recognize the demands the milieu makes of them. Generally the audience for outdoor performance will congregate on three sides of an open space. That's not a law but it happens more often than not especially when the performers exercise some choice in targeting their stage area. Generally, when performing before a crowd of people—some milling, some passing by—at various distances from the place of the core performance activity, remember that only the front row can see the actors. While this should encourage the actors to develop a performance that plays high—even over the heads of the audience, below the waist is sure to be a dead area handicapped by very poor sight lines. Because people are preoccupied, their attention has to be drawn to the performance. People are busy. They have lives to lead. Only a select few will give up time to attend an educational event voluntarily. Most will want to be entertained. And if that entertainment can come to them free, so much the better.

Street theatre is a generic term for all manner of performances conducted where people are on the street or in the marketplace. Performances can be short and impromptu, developing with interaction with the watching crowd, or they can be slightly extended and carefully scripted and rehearsed. But they always operate on the assumption that the audience can leave, and that at least some of the members of the audience may leave during the performance. It is up to the performers to get people's attention and then to keep it longs enough to convey their message. Often the people are alert...they are informed and the play only goes to add new dimensions or perhaps the play is a call to wake them from their sleep. "It must be kept in mind that the spectators are always in their senses" as Dr. Johnson in his 'Preface to Shakespeare' (1765)[6] put it or as even Coleridge suggested that "true stage-illusion in this and in all other things consists—not in the mind's judging it to be a forest, but in its remission of the judgement that it is not a forest."[7] Yet the better playwright sees to it that the effect does not run loose...but that he is able to retain 'control.' Ibsen in that sense has been a master dramatist who was able to comprehend the distinctive virtues of audience participation common to all drama.

Street plays involve the spectator to the extent that they make him an ideal 'producer' in his imagination. A play has the cathartic effect on the audience that makes him take 'momentous decisions of will' (Dr. I.A. Richards, *Practical Criticism*, 305).[8]

Some very hilarious street plays have been written, *e.g.* the one authored by Statesman News Service, Publication: *The Statesman*, Calcutta Dated: Aug. 21, 1999 that focuses on Mrs. Sonia Gandhi's struggles with the intricacies of Hindi and the players lend themselves easily to her rivals' campaign. In the play linguistic errors, real and imagined, have found their way into the Nukkad Natak (street-corner theatre) called *Hamen Rome ka nahin Ram ka Rajya Chahiye*, presented by the Sakriya Natya Manch Actors in the play wore saffron kurtas, but that was not the play's only connection with the colour. The play is critical of the way the Vajpayee government was toppled and of the politicians who brought it down. The audience is shown a pictorial depiction of how the government fell for a single vote. The play begins with a man returning home to tell his wife that he has struck gold as "Madam Dus Numbri" has put him in charge of paying people attending her meetings. The Congress president's Italian origin and inability to master Hindi have been exploited to the hilt. A scene where Mrs. Gandhi visits an Andhra village had the audience in splits. A senior Andhra Pradesh Congress leader dials "420" to get through to 'Madam' and invites her to visit the village. There, she is told that the green chilly crop has failed and her advice to farmers is: grow red chillies. In exaggeratedly accented Hindi, Mrs. Sonia Gandhi demands to know where the village beauty parlour is, where the nearest swimming pool is, where she can get mineral water. She visits the 'Rahul Gandhi Open University'—a building without a roof. Told that the villagers are waiting for her speech, she says, "Main garib ko Khatam kar doongi" (I will finish the poor), then attributes it to a typographical error in the Roman Hindi script of her written speech.

The above example of piercing humour involves the entire audience that is well versed with the political scenario. Similarly human rights activists, students activists and women activists of various ideologies have used the street theatre effectively. Since 1992 the rural peasant women animators of the GDS (Organization of the Poor from the Mountain) have presented a street play, all written by them. Dialogues, songs, and scenario with no written text expose the basic reasons for the rejection of wives by their husbands—such as they see and analyze them. The direction was entirely theirs. When this play was staged at Aurangabad in 1994, the audience listened to and followed the play, flabbergasted. The scenes from real life that were presented visibly upset women from the audience. Many of them, who had come from areas that were far away, sang in chorus with the actresses, the songs of the millstone that the latter had taken up for accompanying and commenting on the scenes that they presented. A number of women in tears were incapable of saying a word; their hands were shaking. They found it necessary to touch each other in order to express and share their emotion, a gesture of reciprocal confession from those with a common destiny.

To conclude I would like to quote J.L. Styan once again (*ibid.*, 289)[9] where writing about the effective role of the playgoer he says that going to a play is not thought of as an escape, certainly not a matter of living life at second-hand "Happily we have a consuming curiosity about man, about his life, his problems, his loves and sorrows and aspirations, the whole range and the sweep of human relationships and conflicts. The audience participates in a way as to come to terms with life. He says, "It is exciting first hand work, and an urgent part of living."

References

1. Styan, J.L., *The Elements of Drama*, Cambridge University Press, 1967, 285.

2. Brecht, B., A Short Description of a New Technique of The Art of Acting which Produces an Effect of Estrangement, Le Theatre dans le monde, IV, 1 (1954).
3. *Ibid.* (Styan, J.L.).
4. http://geocities.com/eufortress.
5. Neelu Kang.
6. Johnson, *Preface* to Shakespeare (1765).
7. Coleridge, The Progress of Drama (1818) in Literary Remains, Quoted in A. Nicoll, *The Theory of Drama* (1931), 35.
8. I.A. Richards, *Practical Criticism*, 305.
9. *Ibid.* (Styan) 289.

Further Reading:

Dr. J.R. Northam's, Ibsen's Dramatic Method (Faber, 1953).

http://www.covent-garden.co.uk/historieso/swordeaters.html.

http://hypatia.ucsd.edu/~ld/hypatia.html.

http://www.aslan.demon.co.uk/index.

STREET THEATRE IN INDIA: BADAL SIRCAR'S CONTRIBUTION IN THE FORM OF THIRD THEATRE

15

Nivedita Tandon

Indian English Drama has come a long way and Badal Sircar is one of the brightest stars in the constellation of Indian Drama. The importance of the Third Theatre or street theatre and its close proximity with Badal Sircar is an important aspect to discuss.

After Independence, street theatre got a shot in the arm as India decided to follow a democratic form of government where freedom of speech and public expression were guaranteed by the Fundamental Rights of the constitution. The IPTA activitists, who were all in the opposition, found theatre a potent weapon for contacting the people and voicing their opinions.

All over India the fifties and sixties were times of political unrest and social upheaval. Theatre activists were becoming disillusioned with the British conventional theatre. Calcutta led the way in the quest for newer forms of theatre. Revolting against the conservatism and elitism of the proscenium stage, several radical groups started staging plays at street corners and in public parks. There were times when as many as six groups would be performing plays in different parts of a park at the same time. These plays, though theatrically not of a very high quality, helped to create political awareness among the common people.

Several factors were responsible for the rise in popularity of the street theatre. First and foremost the growing unemployment among the educated youth of the lower middle class, and their sense of adventure and exuberance once found expression in street theatre. Secondly the masses were increasingly becoming aware of the growing corruption in public life. In their frustration they turned to street theatre more and more.

Most of the groups behind street theatre were once active in proscenium theatre. Sensing the futility of their effort to reach out to the masses they went in search of a cheap mobile medium that would help them work towards an egalitarian society. This search resulted in street theatre. Street theatre may be seen as an invention precipitated by a necessity or a crisis. It is a modern urbanised version of the numerous folk forms. The possibilities of dynamic improvisations in foık theatre have made street theatre a popular medium.

Various issues of social and ecological concerns are voiced through this medium of theatre. They seek to enlighten the masses on a plethora of social, political, religious, economic, communalism, caste disparities, terrorism, nuclear disasters, corruption, and AIDS awareness find a place in the repertory of street plays.

Street theatre is an effective medium of communication with the masses because it dispenses with the use of elaborate costumes, sets and lights, it is portable, economical and flexible.[1] It is both didactic and simple in the message it delivers. The actors are all activists trying to convert people to their fiercely held conviction of social justice. They do not wait for an audience to come to a theatre to see them. Instead, they go out to the people accosting them at bus stations, street corners and parks where they are forced to take notice. Some merely peen in out of curiosity and move on. Others respond spontaneously, clapping and jovially replying to questions; the actors raised interaction between actor and audience is a crucial part of this medium, for it provides immediate feedback on how the message is being received and how the script needs to be altered before the next performance. The script is never a finished product that the actors have to interpret, but a dynamic entity that changes from performance to performance depending on the audience it feeds.

As a theatre of protest, street plays come into their own at times of social and political upheaval. In the euphoria following independence, street theatre sank into abysmal depths, until the disillusionment of the sixties prompted playwrights to start reviving it in West Bengal. Badal Sircar was perhaps the first playwright to abandon the stage for the street. This experimental form involved a minimum use of dialogue (to avoid the disturbance of street and traffic sounds) and an emphasis on dramatic, stylised movements that communicated more effectively than words.

Badal Sircar effectively transcends the confines of the urban commercial theatre and indigenous folk theatre. The third theatre aims at changing the thoughts and beliefs of the spectators and leading them to some action. The third theatre dispenses with all stage paraphernalia and lays stress on the most essential tool; the human body. It is literally a free theatre in the sense that no tickets are sold. It is a living experimental communication between the performer and the spectator where the plays become a participatory ritual. What Sircar wishes to communicate through his Third Theatre are clear art facts and concrete truths about what is happening in the villages at the grass roots level, the nature of exploitation, both industrial and agricultural, and the urban strange hold on the rural economy. The ultimate aim of his theatre is to make people aware.

Badal Sircar's formulation of the Third Theatre led him to produce several plays, the first being Spartacus. The most prominent of Sircar's plays based on the concept of the *Third Theatre are Procession* 1972, *Bhoma* (1974) and *Stale News* (1979). Through his three typical street plays one can see the realization of Sircar's philosophy and vision of making people aware of their social responsibility. He makes theatre a medium of conveying individual responsibility of the people towards the society.

Sircar's 'Procession' is about the search for a "real home"—a new society based on equality. It is about a new society where man does not have to live by exploiting man and in which each works according to his ability and gets according to his needs.

Bhoma is a dramatisation of the life of the oppressed peasant in Indian rural society through a series of scenes in which he is socially and economically exploited. A conscientious playwright not only presents the gravity of the problem but also offers a solution by employing powerful symbols and images. The society full of opportunists and exploiters is presented as a forest of poisonous trees and Bhoma, an aboriginal barbarian as a woodcutter. Bhoma is an archetype of the oppressed exploited peasant who, at long last, takes up his "rusty axe" grinds and sharpens it to cut the poisonous trees that grow around him.

Stale News, which is different from both *Procession* and *Bhoma*, deals with the theme of revolt. It centres round a young man who is bombarded with shattering information full of contradictions and contrasts which come to him as "stale news." Though he becomes aware through the inspiring guidance of the Dead Man of the pathetic conditions of the poor and the need for social reform the young man is not ready to come out of the strange hold of the traditional, routine life and develop a sense of commitment so as to revolt against the social and economic justice.

It is these three plays of Badal Sircar that have placed him on a pedestal higher than other contemporary playwrights of Indian Drama. It is through his form "Third Theatre" Sircar makes the society, especially the middle class feel guilty for being indifferent towards man and his problems.

The characters in his play are not individualised used at all. They can be seen as what Sircar himself has said, "I can be taken as a prototype of a particular class in a society at a particular period."[2] The spectator assumes a protagonists' role in the theatre of Sircar, making the theatrical incident experimental, in determinative and open-ended.

If we look closely at this form "Third Theatre" which Sircar calls his street plays to differentiate from westernized proscenium theatre and traditional folk theatre, but drawing from both, we will see that it has become a force to reckon with. All over India, "Third Theatre" is recognized as the epitome of conscientious and experimental theatre.

Sircar was fully aware of the dichotomy between urban proscenium theatre and traditional rural theatre. He tried to create a theatre of synthesis. The popularity of cinema and television and the attempt of theatre to match that popularity baffled him like Grotowoski, he resorted to the elimination process and asked. "Without the presence of what, can theatre cease to exist?"[3] This helped him to the very core of theatre, avoiding all incidentals like make up, music, costumes, lights, sets and props. He realised that the distinctive nature of theatre is that it is a "live" show which offers scope for a direct person to person communication, involving four distinct forms; performers and performers, performers and spectator, spectator and performer and spectator and spectator.

His convictions led him to minimize and even eliminate the barriers between the performer and the spectators. He broke down the proscenium and experimented with circular staging, without props, sets or stage lights. It was becoming clearer to him that ultimately theatre depended on the performers body and the spectator's imagination. Techniques like the elaborate use of mime, body language, symbols and imageries, stylised movements, human props and chorus singing were tried to enlighten the imagination of the audience. An important means of participation was by urging the audience to concentrate intently on the actions of play, most of which were done in highly imaginative mimes. Direct eye contact with the audience was also encouraged in order to heighten participation.

Sircar also experimented with themes, archetype and stereotypes instead of plots and characters. This is evident from the themes of the plays discussed in the paper.

As Sircar experimented with and was exposed to the works of Schechner, Julian Beck, Judith Malina. Andre Gregory and others he went on to make his theatre increasingly subtle and at times in comprehensible. Into a fragmented script he introduced techniques likes physical acting, stylised movements, chorus of voice, non-verbal sounds, alternative music, rhetorical techniques of dialogue delivery, juxtaposing comments which the actors mouthed mechanically, collages of images and words and the repetition of words to create an effect of incantation. He also adapted the spatial, environmental seating of the audience as propounded by Schechner. Techniques like magical sculpting in space, simultaneous action, lack of time space barriers, slow motion and freeze created the magic of the third theatre. These techniques were closely related to the episodic and fragmented format of the script. Sircar not only created rhythms and choreography but also challenged the inaction and irresponsibility of his audience in a subtle way. All these innovations appealed greatly to the aesthetic canons of his audience who were mostly theatre crazy, urban middle class dilettanti.

Sircar worked to change the contents of his plays drastically. His plays belonging to the third theatre were powerful responses to the various socio-political realities he encountered. These plays show Sircar's deeper understanding of the problems of the nuclear age and of poverty, corruption, greed and the industrial and agricultural exploitation of the poor. Through his novel style of production he asked the audience to face these problems as personal issues and to try to do something about them. The plays were not overtly political but showed the individuals caught in the web of politics. Instead of advocating strikes, lockouts and the overthrow of the government he was content to disturb the conscience of his spectators urging them to contribute their might to reconstructing the state of chaos.

Badal Sircar gave a potent weapon in the hands of the theatre groups by way of his third theatre. It would not be out of place to look into the reasons of emergence of street theatre, the various themes handled in the street theatre and the effect of street theatre.

If we look into the various causes of the emergence of the street theatre what immediately comes to mind is that the main reason was that it was a response to the needs of the time. After Independence India decided to follow a democratic form of government where quarantined by the Fundamental Rights of the constitution; the IPTA activists realised the importance of theatre. The growing discontent of the educated unemployed youth of the lower middle class (who attributed their misery and negligence to those in power) found vent in street theatre.

Secondly street theatre is an effective medium in breaching the cultural barrier which is propagated by the mass media. The cinema has provided escapist entertainment for gullible audience. Much of the conventional theatre is but a poor imitation of films as a result, traditional values family relationships, religion and respect for elders are being destroyed. But at the same time, in the rural areas and among reactionary groups, these traditional values survive intact. These reactionary groups find their expression by way of the street theatre.

Much of street theatre echoes the sentiments of the public. Some of them treat it as pure love of theatre, for others it is an expression of responsible citizenship in developing the consciousness of uneducated masses. Environmentalists and ecologists, people fighting for women's rights and other concerns like child and bonded labour and civil rights strongly believe that street theatre is the ideal platform for them. They argue that they have a role to play as citizens, as privileged people with education to enlighten the masses on issues that are important.

Street theatre provides an outlet for those involved in experimental theatre as it encourages participatory performances of small groups. Initially it was Sircar who began experimenting with theatre forms. Today there are a number of groups who perform in halls for small audience. Probir Guha works in the living theatre of Kharadah is one that comes readily to mind experimenting with the expressive skills and techniques of traditional forms like chaau, jatra, baul singing, Kalari payattu and other forms of martial arts he has developed a skilful form of the theatre that builds on Sircar's experiments.

As for the various themes—the majority of themes are undoubtedly on socio-political issues. Contemporary issues are what make street plays succeed. Given the structure of the street plays it is not difficult to improvise a play on an event that happened only a few hours before. Perennial issues like communalism, terrorism, police brutality, bride burning, dowry system, caste inequalities, industrial and agricultural exploitation, health care and alcoholism are included in their repertory. A major section of street theatre is inspired by leftist ideologies and the expose corruption in government and challenge the established and accepted values and institutions. In this category come plays on the caste system, all forms of exploitation by the powerful, rural poverty, exploitation of women and children, class hierarchies and bonded labour.

The relevance of studying street theatre would be lost if one did not analyse the effect of it on the players, the audience, on the mass media and on the power groups against whom the street theatre targets. In Aristotelian parlance the cathartic effect of poetry can be seen manifesting itself through street theatre. We can see that the purpose of the street theatre is to shake the people out of complacency and make them react against contemporary and topical issues.

As already mentioned the players are from various cross sections; students, unemployed youth, teachers, political activists and people with various other ideologies are involved in this form of theatre.

Working in a street play needs one to maintain a delicate balance between commitment to ones own responsibilities, family relationships and theatre work. At the same time however the street theatre opens up new avenues for observing and understanding people. It also helps define a definite social attitude in the absence of which it becomes difficult to operate as a responsible person. For political activists every performance is a reassertion of the values they stand for.

For the audience the effect is both immediate and delayed. When topical issues are dealt with many audience go out feeling the immediate impact. There have been instances when the audience watching street theatre on themes of partition have sobbed and wept and told the actors "where were you all these years? All that you say is so real and close to our experience and reality."[4]

As for delayed results the audience who witness these plays are the youth, most of the times unemployed youth and the poor who cannot afford costly means of entertainment. They seem to identify with the problems posed in the plays, because street theatre focuses on the dreary side of life and tries to lend a voice against all forms of injustice. Some audience express displeasure at the plays not being as entertaining and versatile as films while some audience are conditioned that the street theatre will analyse serious topical issues. In many places the performances become an event; people talk about it for days. Men debate the pros and cons of the play at tea sessions and evening jaunts, children enact their favourite scenes, recite the dialogues and hum the tunes. This can add up to an ongoing education.[5]

As for the effect on Mainstream Media—the urban proscenium theatre practitioners and other media merchants look down on street theatre practitioners. But the techniques of street theatre as popularised by Sircar have been adapted in several stage plays. Directors such as Faisal Alkazi and Rati Bartholomew have taken to street theatre. In the field of cinema, parallel cinema deals with social issues in a challenging way and success of such films shows the impart in a positive way.[6]

As for the power groups—generally street plays are not aimed at the policy-makers, opinion leaders or power holders. There have been instances of power groups being shaken. Local governments and others in power at times categorize theatre activities as subversive activity. Instances of police intervention to disrupt performances dates back to the early years of IPTA. All over India political plays were fanned and scripts destroyed. Things are changing, the government itself is financing workshops on street theatre and arranging International conferences.

Street theatre has become an important tool to promote awareness in the minds of people on topical and perennial issues.

References

1. Jacob Srampickal, "Street theatre: Protest all the way" in *Voice to the Voiceless* (C. Hurst & COL Pubs. Ltd., UK, 1994), 99-153.
2. Badal Sircar, "Azad Memorial Lectures," 1982 quoted by Ella Dutta in the Introduction to *Three Plays*, V.
3. Jacob Srampickal, "Personal interview with Badal Sircar," Street *Theatre: Protest all the Way*, 106.
4. Tanushree, "Natya Yatra 87" in *Padgham* an occasional news magazine of Nav Nirman Sanskritik Samiti, Bombay 2-2-1987.
5. K. Sumana, "The Importance of Indian Street Theatre with special Reference to the plays of Badal Sircar," *The Commonwealth Review*, Vol. V, No. 1 (1993-94), 61-65.
6. Sudhakar Pandey and Freya Taraporewala (eds.), *Contemporary Indian Drama*, "Experiment and Innovation in Modern Indian Drama in Translation: The Plays of Mohan Rakesh, Badal Sircar and Girish Karnad," 64-72.

TAGORE AND VIJAY TENDULKAR

A BIOGRAPHICAL SKETCH OF TAGORE AND TENDULKAR

16

Neeru Tandon

TAGORE

One of the greatest poets of India, and a man of striking personal appearance R.N. Tagore, the youngest child of *Maharishi Devendranath*, was born on May 7, 1861 in Calcutta. His grandfather Dwarkanath was called the prince because of his lavish style of living. He had amassed much wealth through his business transactions and the Tagores lived in luxury. However the times charged and the prince suffered heavy losses and when he died in 1846 he left the family in debt. R.N. Tagore's father was not only an original thinker and philosopher but also a man of great honesty and integrity, courage and determination. Maharishi, as he was known redeemed the family zamindari by paying off all the debts. The family had recovered from its financial difficulties and was reasonably well off during Rabindranath's infancy. Tagore grew up in very comfortable circumstances although the splendours of the days of the prince were gone. Their family mansion in Jorasanko, Calcutta was spacious and comfortable and the family maintained a number of servants. As far as material comforts and luxuries are concerned, nothing was lacking which a growing boy can possibly desire.

The Tagore family was educated enlightened and progressive unlike most of the orthodox and superstitious Hindu families. All the family members had literary artistic and progressive taste. Tagore's Jorasanko home was the centre of theological, political, artistic, literary and other cultural activities. Rabindranath's eldest brother, Dwejendranath was a philosopher and possessor of a prose style adequate to his thought, another brother Jyotindranath was an amateur artist, Satyendranath the second brother was the first Indian to enter the Civil Services.

So, Rabindranath, from his earliest days, grew up in one house where all the surging tides of the Indian Renaissance could flow round his daily life and fill the air breathed with the exhilaration of their fresh airs. R.N. Tagore, however was a lonely child, who had to fall back for most of the time on his own resources. His mother was more or less an invalid, and her domestic duties left her with no time for the child. His father was too busy to come close to the growing child and give him that love and affection for which his soul hungered. He was chiefly looked after by the servants who did not allow him to go out of the house.

Rabindranath's education began quite early and he was put to various schools in Calcutta. He did not care much for the school curriculum and his reading was largely haphazard. Practically speaking, his education was largely self-education. About his schooling in Calcutta, he speaks with disgust and the time he spent there was a penal servitude for him. At home he was educated by his brother Hemendranath, but he was disgusted with his rigid discipline, which education in those days implied. So at the age of 17 in 1878, he was sent to London where he studied for sometime in the University of London under Prof. Henry Morley, for whom he has expressed genuine admiration. He returned to India in 1880. However, he was again sent to England in 1881, with the intention of studying law. But he went only upto Madras, and returned home from there. There was no further attempt to educate him in the conventional manner. Tagore picked up knowledge at home with phenomenal quickness. His natural passion for poetry, music, acting and art led him to master all that was connected with them. As he was a keenly observant boy, he could get much valuable education from the world around him and from the world of nature. There was much artistic cultural and literary activity in the home itself and he could imbibe much from the discussions on various subjects which were a daily feature in the Tagore mansion. He had notable experiences, which expanded and uplifted his mind and spirit. His father, an incessant traveller, took the boy Tagore with him. He stayed for sometime at Bolpur (1873), which today is world-famous for his school and retreat (Shantiniketan).

The most dominant influence in his boyhood days, on him was that of his brother Jyotindranath's wife, Kadambri Devi. She was an enlightened lady, progressive in her views and interested in art and literature. She was a sympathetic friend and companion to the lonely child, whom she encouraged to think and feel in his own way. After the death of his mother in 1875, she was something of a mother to the poor orphaned boy, and when Rabindra began to write she was his first admirer and sympathetic critic. She saved him from the faults of vanity and lack of self-criticism.

Tagore was married to Mrinalini Devi in December, 1883 and his brother's wife Kadambri Devi died in May 1884. A year after his marriage he became the secretary of the Adi Brahmo Samaj of which his father was the most important leader. As his mind had no intellectual narrowness and as his heart was full of love, he was able to rise above all petty man made barriers between two religions. His mystical vision had enabled him to see the inner spiritual significance of much that a hard-headed and hard-hearted man might brush aside as idolatry, theology or metaphysics. In him it was the Hindu genius that was predominant and irradiated everything. He was a ceaseless critic of the Hindu caste system, and as the secretary of Adi Brahmo Samaj he registered his protest against it by asking non-Brahmins to come and preach and deliver sermons from its platform.

His father, noticing his contemplative and reserve nature and his habit of seclusion and aloofness, sought to wean him away from such undesirable tendencies, by asking him to shoulder family responsibility. In 1901 R.N. Tagore made a new experiment in the field of education. His father had bought a large plot of land near Bolpur, which he called Shantiniketan. It was a quiet place in the midst of natural surroundings. Here the poet established the Bolpur

Brahmacharyashram which afterwards developed into the Vishva-Bharati. Vishva Bharati was formally inaugurated in 1921 and was intended to be a seat of international learning and aimed at a synthesis of Eastern and Western cultures. He felt that India, and more particularly Bengal, was afflicted with the worst system of education in the whole of the British empire, and it was his purpose to establish a school in harmony with the national tradition and close to nature. In this period, between 1901 and 1907, he became a serious novelist, and wrote *Gora*, the greatest novel in Bengali.

In 1909 Tagore published Gitanjali in Bengali, in 1912 he went to England and published English translation of *Gitanjali*. In 1913 he was awarded the Nobel Prize for literature on the basis of the English version of his *Gitanjali* that made him an international figure and a celebrity. He was greatly honoured wherever he went. An honorary doctorate was conferred on him by Calcutta university the same year. In 1914 he was knighted. The *Gitanjali* and the *Post Office* marked a great transition in his life when the Tagore's national longing became merged in the universal. But very soon this longing and enthusiasm disappeared but he continued to write essays, poems and short stories. In 1915 Gandhiji visited Shantiniketan to meet Tagore (Gurudev); where the poet gave him the title 'Mahatma.' In 1916, he published *Phalguni* (or The cycle of Spring). It became famous as a musical drama.

In Tagore's personal life 1902-1907 were the fatal years. His wife Mrinalini died in 1902. His youngest son, Sami, died in 1907. It continued till 1918 when his daughter Bela died after a long illness. In 1918, he published *Palatake* (or The Runaway) which proved to be his last collection of verse. In 1919, Tagore renounced the knighthood because of Jallianwala Bagh Massacre in Amritsar.

Tagore was the cultural ambassador of India so he delivered many lectures and speeches in Eastern and Western countries dwelling upon the glory and greatness of our ancient culture. He raised India's image wherever he went. He produced his autobiography Jivansmriti in 1912 and its English version, *My Reminiscenes* appeared in 1917. According to him life's history may be termed autobiography but life's memories may be called reminiscences. Tagore's reminiscences are purely personal and subjective and they deal with the growth of his poetic genius. *Chhelebeha*, a collection of Tagore's memoirs from his earliest recollections to his first trip abroad in 1878, was published in 1940. It was rendered into English by Marjorie Skykes as 'My Boyhood Days.' In it he mentions some new details which were left out in *My Reminiscences*. There is greater candidness and intimacy in *My Boyhood Days* than in *My Reminiscences*.

Tagore dedicated the last twenty years of his life to Visvabharati, which was formally inaugurated on 22nd December, 1921. Tagore's dream of a world university came true with Visvabharati. It was a meeting place for diverse peoples and cultures. Another bright aspect of Rabindranath Tagore appeared as a painter. He inaugurated an exhibition of his pictures in Paris in May 1912, followed by exhibitions of his paintings at Copenhagen, Moscow and other places. His pictures were admired by some for their dreaminess and the atmosphere of mystery they evoke as well as by the technical excellence which they display. Satyajit Ray wrote, "It is important to stress that [Tagore] was uninfluenced by any painter, eastern or western. His work does not stem from any tradition but is truly original. Whether one likes it or not, one has to admit its uniqueness." Ananda Coomaraswamy, the best known critic of Indian art, had written, "The poet (Tagore) gives no descriptive titles to his pictures—how could he? They are not pictures about things, but pictures about himself...any method of (painting) is employed that may be available or that may suggest itself at the moment. The artist, like a child, invents his own technique as he goes along; nothing has been allowed to interfere with zest."

The Calcutta university had already conferred on him the Doctorate of Literature Honoris Causa and he had delivered a series of lectures on poetics there. The University of Oxford also arranged a special convocation at Shantiniketan on 7th August, 1940 to confer on him an honorary Doctorate of

Literature. It was the first time when the Oxford University had travelled to confer a degree.

Tagore left behind him an immense mass of prose writing in Bengali as well as in English but undoubtedly Tagore was a poet and other writings are but the by-product. Next only to *Gitanjali* perhaps, *The Gardener* is the richest of the collections that have appeared in English.

In 1940 Tagore fell seriously ill, and finally on the 7th August 1941, this myriad-minded man breathed his last. His place in the field of Art, Music and Literature is secured and assured. Chaudhuri rightly wrote, "I would loudly proclaim that the status of Rabindranath as a literary man was higher than that of all the thirteen Western writers who had received the Noble Prize from 1901 to 1912." As a humanist and redeemer of spirituality, Tagore's place is very high in modern world. It has been rightly said, by *Ortega Y. Gasset.*

> That voice of Tagore, from where does it come?
> Does it come from the East or from the West?
> Does it come from near or from far away?
> We do not know. Rather it seems to come
> Simultaneously from the round line which forms
> the horizon of life.

The Main Works of Tagore

Rabindranath Tagore, the most outstanding name in modern Bengali literature, had a mastery of English also. He translated many of his poems and plays into English. He also lectured in English to audiences outside India or outside Bengal, and he also wrote many letters in English. That's why he also belongs to Indian literature in English. His fecundity and vitality were amazing. His active literary career extended over a period of 65 years. In Bengali, there are twenty-eight large volumes consisting of poetry, dramas, operas, short-stories, novels, essays and diaries, and a similar number of volumes of letters, still being edited and published. His songs, separately published are nearly two and a half thousand in number, his paintings and drawings are over two thousand. A large fraction of all this is still read, performed and studied in

Bengal. He was a poet, dramatist, actor, producer, musician, painter, educationist, practical idealist, social reformer, philosopher, prophet, novelist, a short story writer, and also a critic of life and literature. Popularly known as GURUDEV, he wrote probably the largest number of lyrics ever attempted by any poet. He began his literary career by writing in Bengali. 'BANPHUL' is his first verse narrative. He emerged as the major Indian writer in English. In fact his work in English is mainly an introduction to his Bengali writings—It is both an invitation and a foretaste. While rendering his poems and plays into English, Tagore often made drastic alterations, curtailments, telescopings. Works like *Gitanjali*, *The Gardener*, and *The Fugitive*, *Chitra*, *The Post Office* and *Sacrifice* compel laudation as English poetry and drama. His novels and the short stories are among the most valuable by-products turned out by the great creative forge of Rabindranath Tagore.

Poetry

Gitanjali (1912)
The Gardener (1913)
The Crescent Moon (1913)
100 poems of Kabir, Translated into English by Tagore (1914)
Fruit-Gathering (1916)
Stray Birds (1916)
Lover's Gift and Crossing (1918)
The Fugitive and other Poems (1921)
Poems from Tagore (1922)
Sheaves: Poems and Songs (1951)
The Golden Boat (1933)
A Flight of Cranes (1953)
The Herald of Spring (1960)
Wings of Death (1960)

Prose Fiction

Hungry Stones and Other Stories (1916)
Mashi and Other Stories (1918)

The Home and the World (Novel)	(1919)
The Wreck (Novel)	(1919)
Gora (Novel)	(1923)
Broken Toys and Other Stories	(1925)
Two Sisters (Novel)	(1944)
Farewell My Friend; and The Garden	(1956)
Binodini (Novel)	(1959)
Four Chapters (Novel)	(1960)
Chaturanga (Novel)	(1963)
The Runaway and Other Stories	(1960)

Plays

Sanyasi or the Ascetic	(1884)
Nalini	(1884)
Mayar Khela	(1888)
The King and the Queen	(1889)
Visarjan	(1890)
Chitra	(1894)
Matine	(1896)
Gandhari's Prayer	(1897)
Karna and Kunti	(1897)
The King of the Dark Chamber	(1914)
The Post Office	(1914)
Sacrifice and Other Plays	(1917)
The Cycle of Spring	(1917)
The Curse at Farewell	(1924)
Red Oleanders	(1925)
Three Plays (Mukta-Dhara, Natir Puja and Chandalika)	(1950)
Devouring Love	(1961)

Thus, undoubtedly, Tagore is a prolific, writer and few can be compared to him in literary output. His works include more than a thousand poems, two thousand songs, innumerable stories, plays, novels, operas, and articles on a wide range of subjects such as education and learning, social reforms, ethical problems etc., which are qualitatively valuable as well. Since his works are mainly in Bengali and have not been adequately translated, therefore, Tagore has not got the apt recognition in the world which he rightly deserves. At the ripe age of seventy he began to paint and in course of ten years he produced three thousand paintings and some of them are marvellous indeed.

VIJAY TENDULKAR

Vijay Tendulkar was born in a Brahmin family on 7th January 1928. He wrote his first play while still in school and later worked as an apprentice in a bookshop. He took up journalism and was an assistant editor of Marathi dailies line *Navbharat*, *Maratha* and *Loksatta*. Tendulkar has written plays, short stories, features and television serials in Hindi. Recipient of many prestigious awards like Kamladevi Chattopadhyaya award, Sangeet Natak Akademi award and Kalidas Samman award, he is fighter for cultural freedom, the freedom which is stifled at present by various forces. Tendulkar has changed the form and pattern of Indian drama by demolishing the three-art play and creating new models. He is noted for criticizing the hypocrisies, promiscuity, dishonesty and such other vices existing in the society.

Tendulkar's 'Ghashiram Kotwal' was first performed on 16 December 1972 at the Bharat Natya Mandir, Pune, by the Progressive Dramatic Association and published in 1973. It won several awards in 1972-73 at Maharashtra State Drama Competition. But after nineteen performances it was banned. Most of the actors resigned and formed Theatre Academy on 27 March 1973. The production was revived on 11 January 1974 and has subsequently been performed extensively by the groups in India and abroad.

Vijay Tendulkar is India's leading contemporary Indian playwright is also well-known as screen and television writer, literary essayist, political journalist and social commentator. A lifelong resident of the city of Bombay, Mr. Tendulkar is the author of thirty full-length plays and twenty-three one-act plays, several of which have become classics of modern Indian theatre. Mr. Tendulkar's output in Marathi also includes eleven plays for children, four collections of short stories, one novel, and five volumes of literary essays and social criticism all of which have contributed to a remarkable transformation of the modern literary landscape of Maharashtra and of India as a whole. He is an important translator in Marathi, having rendered nine novels and two biographies into the language, as well as five plays, among which are Mohan Rakesh's 'Adhe Adhure' (Hindi), Girish Karnad's 'Tughlaq' (Kannada), and Tennessee Williams' 'A Street Car Named Desire' (English). He is the author of original stories and screenplays for eight films in Marathi, including *Samana* (Confrontation, 1975), *Simhasan* (Throne, 1979), and *Umbartha* (The Threshold, 1981), the last a groundbreaking feature film on women's activism in India.

During the 1970s and 1980s he wrote the original scripts and dialogue for eleven Hindi films among them *Nishant*, *Manthan*, *Akrosh*, *Ardhya-Satya* and *Aghat*—which define the paradigm for the 'Middle-Cinema' movement in India, positioned between the art Cinema of such film makers as Satyajit Ray, and the commercial cinema produced by Bollywood. In addition, he has written and directed discussion—shows on current social issues for Indian television in Hindi.

Mr. Tendulkar's dramatic output and theatrical activities in Marathi and his work in Hindi Cinema have received wide recognition, bringing him the Maharashtra State Government Award (1956, 1969, 1973), the Sangeet Natak Akademi Award (1971) and the Filmfare Award for the best Screenplay for 'Akrosh' in 1980, and for 'Ardhya-Satya' in 1983. His lifetime achievement in the literary and performing arts has been recognized by the Government of India's 'PADMA BHUSHAN (1984), the Maharashtra Gaurav Puraskar (1990), the Janasthan Award (1991), the Kalidas Samman (1992). The Pandit Mahadev Shastri Joshi Award (1999) and the Dinanath Mangeshkar Award (1998).

Among his other honors are a Nehru Fellowship (1973-74), an Honorary Doctorate from the Ravindra Bharati University, Calcutta (1992), and a Lifetime Fellowship from the National Academy of the performing Arts, New Delhi (1998).

He is the co-founder and president of the experimental theatre group, Avishkar (Bombay) and has served on the Board of Directors of the National School of Drama (New Delhi) and the Bharat Bhavan Rangmandal (Bhopal). He has been a member of the Advisory Council of the Shriram Centre of the Arts (New Delhi), a trustee of the National Book Trust (New Delhi), as well as the President of the National Centre for Advocacy Studies (Pune).

INSIGHT INTO FEMININE MIND: A STUDY OF TAGORE'S DRAMATIC WORLD

17

B.R. Agrawal

Women in literature, through the centuries, have been based upon the mythic models from the *Ramayana* and the *Puranas*: Sita—the silent sufferer, the archetype of Indian womanhood; the Earth—Mother, forbearance personified; Savitri—the devotion and dedication incarnate, woman as mother and protector, woman as inspirer and cherisher, woman as the motivating primal force—"Shakti" protecting good and destroying evil, or woman as charmer or lurer. Womanhood in all its variety is equated with selflessness, powerlessness, chastity, docility, virtuosity etc.—that are quite antagonistic to 'me-ness', autonomy and self-definition. Simone de Beauvoir is of the view that the history of humanity is a history of systematic attempt to silence the female. She states, "One is not born, but rather becomes a woman. It is civilization as a whole that produces this creature...which is described as feminine."[1] But the present concept is altogether changed, though our lot is different from that of the western culture and literature. The process of change has been slow and *Woman's Liberation Movement* supported the upliftment of woman in society. During colonial rule in India, there was an awareness of the need of improvement in women's condition and the idea to impart education to women was revived. The birth of two movements *i.e.* Social Reform Movement and Nationalist Movement during the 19th century had deep impact on the status of women. Indian woman's freedom from the shackles of illiteracy and ignorance symbolically as well as literally heralded the dawn of Independence. Tagore feels the undeniable presence of women in society and their significant role. In one of his discourses on *Women's Place in the World* he owes his endless debt to womankind specially to those women who helped him in shaping his dreams and destiny. "They came to me as the seasons come to the earth, with varied urgings of flowers and fruitfulness; they brought to my life, the inspiration of love and beauty, invocation of the power that lies dormant until touched by womanly grace."[2] His plays are unconventional in portraying women and here he surpasses Bankim Chandra and Sarat Chandra.

Rabindra Nath Tagore was the most brilliant creative genius of the Indian renaissance, less a philosopher—more a visionary, maker of modern Indian literature, indispensable to aesthetic education, a genuine nationalist and a world man. He preferred values; as a visionary he sought to foresee the future. His non-conformism was more radical and consistent that made him a fearless critic of social practices and religious beliefs, such as, denunciation of caste system, the world-denying streak of ascetics, the role of priests etc. He was deeply acquainted with Sanskrit Classics, Bengali Literature, English Literature and Continental European Literature. Out of his father's spiritual legacy and moral earnestness and his grandfather's spirit of enterprise, he created his own artistic sensibility. He enriched every genre of literature as a restless experimenter and innovator in the field of poetry, novels, plays, short stories, essays, literary criticism, polemical writing, travelogues, memoirs etc.; he created his own genre of dance drama. His plays are basically expressions of the soul's quest for beauty and truth. There are certain traditional national attitudes; some unshakable obscure racial memories and quite a few perennial recurrent archetypal human patterns and these are the stuff out of which he creates his dramatic world. M.K. Naik divides his plays, thematically into two broad groups: thesis plays and psychological dramas.

The making of an artist owes immensely to the milieu, the socio-political factors which shape his thoughts and sensibility. Tagore too was confronted with the evils of British imperialism: the fearful economic scenario and ignorance of the masses, violation of the freedom of press, glaring social injustice and heinous caste-system, sati-system, polygamy, miserable plight of widows etc. A torch of social reformation was shown by Raja Ram Mohan Roy and Bankim Chandra. Tagore's writings exhibit the same democratic enlightenment and nationalistic fervour. The direct reflection of feudal obscurantism is reflected in the terrible condition of women in society. Tagore believed in progress and prosperity of humanity as a whole, he succeeded in avoiding the influence of the liberals and had no illusions about a special patriarchal development. The progressive and feminist outlook of Tagore espousing women's emancipation was not only the result of his personal thinking it imbibed also the progressivist thinking of the west. He seems to promote a dynamic code of relation based on the ideal of democracy and humanism. The circumference of human relationship determined by society is significant only to the extent that they do not diminish the eternal glory of human spirit. Therefore, he seems to be attempting a compromise between Indian Tradition and Western Culture in delineating the various aspects of man and woman interaction and specially in ascribing various roles and responsibilities to women.

Like Raja Ram Mohan Roy and Ishwar Chandra Vidyasagar, Tagore seems to be the champion of the emancipation of women. Most of his works concentrate on the plight of widows, the anxiety of modern educated woman for equality and freedom, the complications arising out of prevalent orthodoxy and conservatism, and the social problems inflicting the mental domain of the fair sex. He delineates the inner-workings and crisscross movements of this section of society with his poetic imagination and psychological insight. His novels unfold a vast range of women-crooked as well as ideal, sweet young as well as adult, traditional as well as assertive and possessive. In the portrayal of the miserable plight of widows like Binodini and Damini, Tagore resembles Sarat Chandra. His stories demonstrate the tragic condition of the women in the feudal backwardness of the society, revealing the cruel exploitation, injustice and absurdity. A study of Tagore's dramatic world reveals the finality of his creativity, innovation and experimentation. It is the culmination of his quest that establishes besides so many things, his venture to recognize the status of women in society, which M.K. Naik calls "Tagore's insight into the feminine mind."[3] He probed into deeper recesses of woman's mind and presented a wide range of women characters. The women characters of his plays represent different facets of Indian womanhood, as varied as life itself. His vast range comprises women who symbolize humanity, love and beauty like—Vasanti, Malini, Nandini and Aparna; ideal women who embody nature and epitomize the beauty and splendour of the earth like Chitra, (Nandini) and Prakriti. If there are traditional women—silent submissive and manifestations of Earth-like magnanimity in their motherhood like Kunti, Gandhari, there are women who are bold and defiant, selfish and assertive like—Gunwati, Sumitra and Devyani (as well as Nandini). Tagore resembles Sarat Chandra Chatterjee in portrayal of women who are exploited and humiliated in the name of tradition and religion. Under the influence of western education and growth of social consciousness, Tagore's women too assert their individuality and fight for their right to love and family happiness. Gunwati is self-centred and assertive and she becomes morally blind. Moral insensitiveness, indifference to other's pain are in view of Tagore the root of folly. By the turn of 19th century, the rapid stride in women education brought to the fore a class of women not prepared to accept the moral and social code of the decadent male-dominated bourgeois society, asserting their individuality and fighting for the equality of sexes as revealed through the character of queen Sumitra, Devyani and Nandini. If woman as a source of creation and inspiration and 'a divine energy' is epitomized in 'Sati' and Malini; Srimati of *Natir Puja* exemplifies in her life and deeds the majesty of the human spirit which refuses to be cowed down by the tyranny of authority and power. A detailed analysis of his dramatic world reveals his insight into feminine mind. On the basis of the varied facets of Indian womanhood they represent, his wide range of women characters can be better divided into the following groups:

(A) Women: Epitome of Humanity, Love and Beauty

In *Sanyasi* (Prakitir Pratishodh) Tagore belittles the life of renunciation and upholds, the dignity of everyday life. He himself says about this play: "It may be looked upon as an introduction to the whole of my future literary work, or rather, this has been the subject on which all my writings have dwelt the joy of attaining the Infinite within the finite."[4] Vasanti the female protagonist of the play, makes the Sanyasi realize that true freedom lies in love and not in emptiness of soul and hatred of worldly things. It is through the love of the little girl that the contempt of the ascetic is transformed into love. In *Sanyasi,* the girl Vasanti is portrayed by Tagore as symbol of humanity and love. Sanyasi, by rejecting her rejects the universal love. She asks for bread, but in his obtuseness he gives her a stone instead. Yet the girl awakens in his heart the dormant springs of humanity. Vasanti's little trusting hand seems to touch his soul with the wand of the eternal, 'She is to him the moth of the day light.' Before Sanyasi adopts her lessons, she is dead. And Tagore questions if the giver of new life to the Sanyasi be really dead? But her death enables him to awaken from the nightmare of egotistic possessiveness and go through the baptism of regeneration as a human being. She symbolizes that true love far from binding, can emancipate and enlarge. She is the vehicle of Tagore's basic tenet of life that love liberates, purifies and intensifies human understanding and reveals infinity in a grain of sand, and heaven in a flower. In one of his lectures on *Woman's Place in the World,* Tagore speaks of woman's capability to "impart her life-rhythm to this reckless movement of power" in today's world. He says, "Her exuberance of vital interest is spontaneously expressive: it makes her speech, her laughter, her movement, graceful and picturesque...."[5]

Malini, too, suggests the triumph of the spirit of love over the spirit of hatred. Through Malini, Tagore conveys the idea that this world is full of religious bigotry and blind fanaticism but there are people like Malini who show to the humanity the path of love in the midst of darkness. Malini is meant by Tagore to be new revelation—'forgive, whatever the crime!

Killing doesn't mend anything.' She requests not to let even the fanatic killer die but have a chance to repent and see things in a new way. Malini is portrayed by Tagore to throw this challenge at us as the Buddha did, as Christ did. We may not be able to rise to her heights, but Tagore did not intend to drag her somehow to our level, and wonder whether she loves Supriya or Kemankar and what conflict in her mind inspires her to this nobility. Malini is, in deed, the new revelation as in her own day in her own way John the Maid was in France. Malini questions Supriya about Kemankar, and later when she sees him in chains, appreciates his unyielding zeal. But she rises far above these mundane considerations when she speaks to Supriya after hearing the tale of Kemankar's betrayal: "Why did you forget yourself, Supriya? Why did fear overcome you? Have I not room enough in my house for him and his soldiers?"[6] And in this connection, Prof. Iyengar's comments on Malini are noteworthy "It is the house of love infinite in dimension, reared on utter fearlessness, walled up by continual understanding and forgiving: canopied by compassion.[7] In Malini, Tagore has presented his ideal concept of womanhood, as "Shakti" the living symbol of divine energy whose inner shrine is in the subconscious depth of human nature and outer manifestations in sweetness of service simplicity, of self dedication and silent heroism of daily scarifies. Tagore probes into the inner working of her heart which is full of love, forgiveness, she knows that she could have won the battle of love openly and effected a change of heart even in Kemankar. That is why she questions the betrayal of Supriya. Therefore her innate divinity and love makes her ask the king to spare Kemankar in the end.

In the companion play *Sacrifice*, Tagore creates Aparna as an emblem of love and duty. Through her appeal, the king has a realization of the heinousness of the practice of animal sacrifice. She acts as the chorus and agent of conversion: it is also the manifestation of the aggressive character of Queen Gunwati. Aparna and Queen Gunwati represent two aspects of the character of a woman. Aparna is in the background all the time. Tagore has skilfully delineated Vasanti, Malini and

Aparna as symbols of humanity, love and beauty. Their innate goodness triumphs over the cruelty, hatred and arrogance of the world.

(B) Women: Embodiment of Nature

Chitra is Tagore's attempt to justify the role of woman, not only as a beautiful agent of Nature but also an interpreter of truth. Tagore's Chitra is like Kalidasa's Shakuntala, epitome of youth, love and romance. Chitra is the quintessence of romance. The speeches burn with passion, and light up the way from truth to illusion, and again the arduous climb from illusion to truth and Tagore portrays Chitra as 'a bare simplicity of truth,' when she throws her ornaments and veils and stands clothed in naked dignity. She is a woman and a mother, and Arjuna is content; he says simply, "Beloved, my life is full."[8] When the borrowed beauty is cast aside, Chitra continues to be graceful as she has known love, because she is now a prospective mother.

Chandalika is not a voice against untouchability rather a story of Prakriti's 'spiritual rebirth,' 'her redemption,' 'a message of liberation' and the second coming of Lord Buddha (in the name of 'Ananda'). Her wild physical desire surrenders before Ananda resplendent with the light of truth; perhaps Tagore wants to highlight the enigmatic character of woman, the character of being all-dominating and over possessive to devour all that stands before her, precisely, her excessive materialistic approach that ultimately fails before spiritual manifestations. Tagore presents a psychological study of a young woman who suffers on account of her vanity and self-consciousness. Her chance meeting with him inflames in her a devouring fire of love which is beyond the understanding of him. But the fever of love captures her and she sends her mother to work the primordial earth spell on Ananda so as to drag him towards her. She succeeds in it but at a heavy cost. Anand is drawn with an irresistible force towards her cottage. But this Anand is not holy and divine-visaged Anand she had cherished, but a miserable sight of fury, agony and storm-smitten one. The very sight draws from her an agonized cry of despair and turns her final victory into her miserable defeat. She helplessly requests her mother:

> Mother, Mother, stop! Undo the spell now-at-once-undo it, what have you done? What have you done? What have you done? O wicked, wicked deed! Better have died. What a sight to see! Where is the light and radiance, the shining, purity, the heavenly glow? How worn, how faded, has he come to my door! Bearing his self's defeat as a heavy burden, he comes with drooping head....[9]

The agony of defeated love and her heart-rending cry has been laid bare before the readers. The retribution takes place in the end with the death of mother, Ananda's release from spell and Prakriti's spiritual rebirth.

Tagore's play *Raktakarabi* (Red Oleanders) was written towards the end of 1923 under the title *Yakshapuri* (The City of Yaksha). On further revising it, Tagore re-titled it as *Nandini* after the name of the female protagonist of the story. [But in 1924, it was further revised to Raktakarabi]. In his preface to the play, Tagore adds a new perspective to the play by referring to the Ravana of Tretayug with enormous ambition and greed, and the appearance of a woman 'Sita' and the demolition of his Swarnlanka. In this play Tagore, too, laments over the exploitative materialistic society's insatiable accumulative instinct and ruthless exploitation of Nature. Here, too, there is a woman 'Nandini' who warns us against man's suicidal violence against Nature. She represents the innocence and opulence of Nature. The call of Paus, the harvesting season, is a call of Nature in her pristine purity and limitless bounty. In the harvesting song which may be regarded as the theme song of the play, Nandini refers to the cosmic harmony of Nature. The song of Nature is a song of selfless love. In the play, Tagore repeatedly tells us that Nandini is the embodiment of Nature. She epitomizes the beauty and splendour of the earth. In midst of the materialistic din, she is always serene, "a finely tuned musical instrument."[10] Sometimes her simple presence becomes a menace to materialism only because of the moral force that she carries about with her. Nandini knows that she is a woman but the fact that she is a woman should not be undervalued. She is like a Nature's lightaning that contains the inherent thunder: "I have brought the thunder, I shall strike the golden citadel,"[11] she says. She is an expression of Tagore's consistent faith that man reflects divinity hence he is an emblem of eternal truth and eternal goodness. Nandini not only denies the authority of the Governor but also expresses indignation towards the divine existence. Tagore's radical attitude echoes through the words of Nandini—"the Gods have all eternity for their worship, they are not pressed for time. But the sorrows of man cannot wait to reach other men, they have so very little time."[12] Tagore himself remarks in his preface about this benevolence and natural majesty of her spirit, "the entire play is an elaborate portrait of Nandini, a woman. She represents the joy of life, the simple beauty and pristine purity of Nature." (Preface) Nandini is presented by Tagore as a spirit of joy, love and beauty. Hers is the challenge of Virgin beauty to the world of male. The professor rhapsodically says:

> She has for her mantle the green joy of the earth. That is our Nandini. In this Yaksha town, there are governors, foremen, headmen, tunnel-diggers, scholars like myself, there are policemen...only she is out of element. Amidst the clamour of the market place, she is a tuned up lyre.[13]

She succeeds in destroying the tyrannical regime in Yaksha town, which has reduced its citizens to gold-digging slaves, though she herself dies in the process.

(C) Woman: As Mother and Protector

If Tagore's women are embodiment of love and humanity, of Nature's spirit, his women manifest Earth mother like magnanimity in their maternal love. A study of his dramatic world reveals that Tagore takes mother and son relationship also as a significant aspect of man-woman relationship. In the plays *Karna and Kunti* and *Gandhari's Prayer*, he dramatizes the inherent properties of this relationship. In these plays, Tagore deals with the conviction that a mother, by nursing a child in her womb, makes the greatest sacrifice and deserves the dues of it. But Tagore's mother characters manifest the truth that the bond of affection determined by birth is not the end of maternal affection. He probes into the mother's psyche and unravels the crisscross movements of their impulses and instincts. Two contrasted manifestations of maternal love are presented in these plays. In *Karna and Kunti*, he portrays Kunti who gave birth to a child before marriage, by blessings of Sun God. She suppresses all her maternal instincts and sentiments and deserts him to avoid social calumny. Karna, brought up by foster parents becomes the leader of Kauravas against the Pandavas (sons of Kunti), in the Mahabharat War. In the play, Tagore dramatizes the moments of intense emotional crises, when Kunti goes to Karna to demand the lease of Arjuna's life. She asserts her lost motherhood and reveals hesitantly her identity to Karna. She admits that because of her cowardice, Karna suffered the pangs of humiliation in society. But the power of her love fails to capture his love and duty. When she fails to persuade Karna by her sentimental appeal, she tempts him of the mighty kingdom. Neither her appeals nor the glamour of kingdom motivate Karna to betray his foster mother. And here Tagore conveys that affection determined by birth can survive only for a definite time. Kunti is told by Karna that the roots of affection of his birth have dried and they cannot be revived by the sudden revelation of 'forgotten motherhood.' "The quick bond of kindred which you severed at its root is dead, and can never grow again.... On the night, of my birth you left me naked and unnamed to disgrace; leave me once again without pity to the calm expectation of defeat and death!"[14]

It is an emotionally pitched soul-searing scene. Kunti, too, is the Mother of Sorrows, she, too, is great because she has suffered as few have ever suffered. And Karna, great and high spirited, like his mother, refuses to be tempted. Now mother and son try to salvage whatever at this late hour is possible from the general wreckage. Kunti remains an adorable woman in Hindu scripture but Tagore's Kunti is a woman with endless tears for her irreparable damage, a capital punishment for a blunder committed unintentionally.

In *Karna and Kunti*, Tagore's attempt seems to highlight the weakness of Kunti and thus establish an ethics for a mother who plays a vital role in social construction beyond all prejudices. In order to establish his ethics, he writes *Mother's Prayer* (Gandhari's Prayer). Here Tagore presents a different view of woman as mother, 'mother of sorrows' reluctant to compromise with evil. She is created by Tagore as an antithesis of Kunti. Gandhari, mother of unjust treacherous Duryodhan steels her heart and requests her husband to renounce their wicked son, Duryodhan who has engineered the exile of the Pandavas through, sheer trickery; and when her prayer is rejected, she prophetically forecasts the terrible day which will bring retribution to all her sons. She is depicted as a great character with a clear vision of the doom to come and she speaks as the 'Mother of sorrows' about the impending disaster when darkness will shroud the sky, earth will tremble, wailing will rend the air. She foresees, also, the silent and cruel end—that terrible peace that great forgetting, and awful extinction of hatred—'the supreme deliverance rising from the fire of death.'

(D) Women: Defiant and Assertive

Most of the times, Tagore rushes to Indian ethos and classics in search of theme and character, to prove his conviction regarding the psychological constitution of woman. But at the same time, he is quite unconventional in portraying women in the tradition of Bankim Chandra and Sarat Chandra. His non-conformism was more radical and consistent with his father's spirit of enterprise. He felt that a patriarchal society is not liberal in conceding its women segment any right and so women's dignity is a glorious exception in a conservative patriarchal set up. Tagore's epoch-making short story '*Streer Patra*' (The Wife Letter) invited protest letters from the conservative sections of society. His progressive and feminist outlook is very well revealed in his plays in the portrayal of defiant and assertive women probably the result of his personal thinking and the progressivist thinking of the west. *The King and the Queen*, the first of his series of tragedies is notable for its success in delineating women, specially Ila, beautiful, loyal a gentle; Queen Sumitra—rare, all pervasive and own-possessive infested with selfish love and yet inviting sympathy for her loneliness suffering and passions. It is queen Sumitra who opens the plot and closes like human life. She is a foil to king Vikram who being infatuated by her love neglects the state and all his obligations towards it. But in Sumitra, Tagore presents a responsible and sensible queen equally cautious towards the call of love and demands of society. She presents Tagore's ideal of modern and dynamic woman. Tagore, nowhere appreciates the suppressed and the subordinated position of woman, rather creates her as a complementary to man. Vikram presents the conventional attitude popular in society. For him man's heart is the only world for a woman; hence as a man he does not reconcile with the dynamic views of Sumitra. He is sure that a lady cannot violate the norms decided by a man. But Tagore never gave himself to conventional ideologies and seems to believe in Shakespearean doctrine of 'marriage of two true minds.' Spirited Sumitra boldly admonishes the king, who lost in his pleasures, neglects his subjects. She will not consent to dwindle into mere mistress and wife, but is ready and eager to bear the responsibilities of a Queen, the patroness of her people. The country is governed by parasites who rebel against the King. Sumitra cannot accept this humiliating position and decides to fight against them, if necessary with help from her brother Kumarsen, Kashmir's King. Here Tagore presents her exemplary courage much in the vein of Nora (though for other reasons) walking out of her husband's house in Ibsen's play. But both she and her brother perish in the ensuing political holocaust. Her defiant words to her hostile husband before her death reveal her spirit, "Sir, no longer your queen: for merciful death has claimed me."[15] The monumental egotism of the king is shattered and the bold queen dominates the play.

In the play *Sacrifice*, Tagore projects a conflict that goes on within the mind of everybody irrespective of any sect or religion, "between temporal and spiritual authority, between brothers and between husband and wife, between humanity and the inhumanity of animal sacrifice before the goddess Kali....[16] Out of these conflicts emerges the conflicting character of woman full of love and hatred, selfish and selfless, rational and superstitious, literally, all the contraries of the world. The play highlights the clash of personal loyalty and professional ethics. Gunwati, being governed by personal interest fails to have on insight into the significance of the decision of her husband. Under the sweep of passions she neglects her duty both as a queen and as a wife. In *King and Queen* the defiance of Sumitra is aimed at rescuing the nation from the orthodox king's negligence. But here Gunwati puts up an arrogant defiance to continue an inhuman custom, which is detrimental for the whole society. And Tagore through her character-analysis presents his regret over the perverted assertiveness and defiance of Gunwati. The queen can think only of the anticipated joys of motherhood. She sends "red bunches of hibiscus and beasts of sacrifice"[17] to be offered to the dread mother, Kali and Raghupati, the orthodox priest assures her that the queen's sacrifice would please the Goddess. He conspires with the queen to dwarf the liberal king's plan to abolish the practice of sacrifice, until the priest's own son, Jai Singh immolates himself on the altar. Raghupati realizes at last the vanity of priestly megalomania and the criminal folly of blood sacrifice. Even Gunwati is redeemed, for the old Goddess is no more—'She has burst her cruel prison of stone and come back to the woman's heart.[18] Gunwati is depicted by Tagore as a good woman within limits, but frustration gives her life a wrong turn. She becomes morally blind, piles blunder upon blunder, and is partly instrumental in driving Jai Singh to suicide. Moral insensitiveness, indifference to other's pain, assertion of one's ego—these are in the view of Tagore the root of folly, which is but another word for crime and Tagore has deftly conveyed it through the portrayal of Gunwati.

Devyani of *Kacha and Devyani* (also titled *Vidya Abhishap* or *Farewell Curse*, 1994) is the most assertive woman character of Tagore who refuses to forgive Kacha, a direct assault on guilty Male's ploy. Her curse reflects the strongest character that a woman may have, declining to surrender before the ever-dominating character of male, proving himself by exploiting the prevalent situation in different ways. Devyani finds all her hopes frustrated when she realizes that her playmate Kacha has only gratitude to offer her but no love and lays a curse on him which practically defeats his very purpose in having come to his father for his training.

To justify his progressive and feminist outlook, Tagore looks upon great and bold women of Indian mythology. In his Preface to *Red Oleanders*, Tagore speaks of our great epic Ramayana and compares the "Yakshatown" to the "Swarnlanka" of Ravana which was demolished because of the great woman Sita. If Ravana is an epitome of material power and prosperity and evinces the evils of materialism, Sita, actually a daughter of earth, a "Bhumi Kanya" represents the strength as well as majesty of human soul. She shows a remarkable spirit of defiance against Ravana, the King of Swarnlanka. For Tagore, it implies the triumph of the values of an agricultural society over those of an industrial system through a lone woman's integrity and moral protest. Like Balmiki's epic Tagore's play, too, has a woman, at the centre, who manifests the spirit of defiance against the dictates of this powerful killer. Sita's spirited defiance started the process of and ultimately brought about Ravana's downfall. In Tagore's play it is just a frail girl, the daughter of this earth, symbolically suggested through the ripe-corn-ears colour of her dress, who refuses to comply with the dictates of the Yaksha regime. There is a hint towards the end that this refusal will finally snowball into a revolution that will shatter the walls of this demonic palace. Nandini, represents the negation of all the values that the Yaksha Kingdom stands for, as Sita rejects the norms (greed-luxury-voluptuousness) of Swarnlanka. Nandini is depicted by Tagore as a defiant lonely woman fighting against the King of dark chambers. By the end of the play, we find that the king has been moved by the spirit of Nandini that there is a clear hint that ultimately the order will be restored and the human values will triumph.

(E) Woman: Triumph of Creation and Inspiration

Tagore, in his plays, has presented his ideal concept of womanhood as motivating 'primal force' as 'Shakti'—the living symbol of divine energy which creates, inspires as well as fights against and triumphs over the evil. In 'Poems' he redefines woman as a source of inspiration and all creativity and calls her epitome of perfect life and thereby signifies the reason behind his inclination:

> Woman, the Sun has tripped you naked, the curse has washed you pure, you have risen into a perfect life...you are young as the new born flowers and old as the hills.[19]

In Malini, Tagore has presented a vision of "Shakti," a symbol of divine energy whose inner shrine is in the subconscious depth of human nature and outer manifestations in sweetness of service and simplicity of beliefs and heroic strength to triumph over the evils of bigotry, fanaticism and orthodox religion and its conventions. She generates love in the heart of orthodox Brahmins, Supriya, Kemankar and everybody. She symbolizes the majesty of human spirit as Srimati in *Natir Puja* does symbolize the affirmation of the spiritual powers of Buddha. Both reveal Tagore's mastery in bringing out the 'blessed eternal feminine.' Tagore gives us a masterly presentation of martyrdom in the character of Srimati, who exemplifies in her life and deeds the majesty of the human spirit which refuses to be cowed down by the tyranny of authority and power. In the climatic scene, Srimati dances before the 'stupa' in a moment of ecstasy, which is an act of sacrilege and painful to her than death which she gladly and religiously accepts. In the ecstasy of dance, she casts away, one by one, the superfluities of jewel and raiment till she is pure and naked in her yellow nun's wrap alone when the guard strikes her dead at the King's command. Tagore makes her present her dance as an act of worship thus establishing her victory in death. Now even queen Lokeshvari and Ratnavali, staunchly opposed to Buddhism, fall upon martyred Srimati's feet muttering:

> I take refuge in the Buddha!
> I take refuge in the Dhamma
> I take refuge in the Sangha

The *Natir Puja* is a real drama of passion and action, where Tagore succeeds in giving a faithful representation of life at a definite period in the history of India. Apart from delineating psychology and majestic spirit of Srimati, the dramatist creates a deep psychological interest in the character of queen mother who is torn between two equally strong impulses—the religious impulse and impulse of womanhood.

To conclude, Tagore's plays cannot be judged on the primary criteria of theme, characterization, social purpose and conflict. His dramatic pursuit is an extension of his poetic expression and lyrical urge. They carry his basic philosophical attitudes and concepts; lyric, emotional and imaginative, brought together with aesthetic harmony. He modified his plays after Shakespeare, Ibsen, Masterlinck, and Kalidas, too. His female characters are vivid and lively. The tragic condition of women in Bengali society was best demonstrated in the feudal backwardness of the society. Revealing the cruel exploitation which women were subjected to during this period, Tagore pointed out the injustice and absurdity of outdated and cruel feudal practices. Tagore's success lies in delineating women than men. His, *Streer Patra* voices protest against marginalisation of woman's rights and interests and the contemptuous refusal to look at her point of view. To justify his stand, he goes to the Hindu scriptures, borrows stories, fits into dramatic framework and presents before us, to revise our opinion about women. The above study of his female characters shows that he has drawn his women with a purpose to stress upon the spiritual powers of love, dignity and grace which they symbolize. With his firm conviction in woman's innate divinity and spiritual power, Tagore has delineated them as an incarnation of the evolution of human love from the physical to the spiritual. They tend to be symbolic and allegorical and sometimes archetypal of humanity, love, beauty and nature's splendour and majesty of human spirit. He fills his dramatic canvass with a wide range of women characters drawn from the society around him and makes them represent varied facets of human life. He is equally well-versed in delineating their maternal sentiments, heartpangs and passions in love, royal assertions, masculine defiance, selfish motives and ego-clashes. Above all, they are firmly rooted in Indian ethos. A study of his dramatic world reveals his deep and uncanny insight into feminine mind.

References

1. Beauvoir, Simone de, *The Second Sex*, transl. and ed. H.M. Parshley, (London: Penguin, 1974), 295.
2. Tagore, Rabindranath, "Woman's Place in the World" in *English Writings of Rabindranath Tagore*, Vol. III ed. Sisir Kumar Das. (New Delhi: Sahitya Academy Edition, 1996), 677.
3. Naik, M.K., *A History of Indian English Literature* (New Delhi: Sahitya Academy, 1992), 102.
4. Tagore, Rabindranath, *Collected Poems and Plays* (London: Macmillan & Co., 1955), 477.
5. Tagore, Rabindranath, "Woman's Place in the World", 677.
6. *English Writings of Rabindranath Tagore*, Vol. II, 89.
7. Iyengar, K.R.S., *Indian Writing in English* (New Delhi: Sterling Publishers Pvt. Ltd., 2002), 130
8. *English Writings of Rabindranath Tagore,* Vol. II, 59.
9. Sykes Marjorie, *Three Plays* (Vishwa Bharati, 1940).
10. Tagore, Rabindranath, *Collected Works of Tagore*, Vol. 6 (Calcutta: Govt. of W. Bengal, 1961), 235.
11. *Ibid.*, 241.
12. *Ibid.*, 249.
13. *Ibid.*, 235.
14. *Collected Poems and Plays by Rabindra Nath Tagore*, 564-65.
15. *English Writings of Tagore*, Vol. II, 129.
16. Ghose, S., *Rabindra Nath Tagore* (New Delhi: Sahitya Academy, 1986), 59-60.
17. *English Writings of Rabindra Nath Tagore*, Vol. II, 89.
18. *Indian Writing in English*, 130.
19. Tagore, Rabindra Nath, *Poems* (Calcutta: Vishwa Bharati, 1943), 16-17.

ROLE OF FREEDOM IN TAGORE'S CONCEPT OF EDUCATION

18

Neeru Tandon

Blessed with a rich and endlessly enviable family background there comes a serene visionary who combines in his educational thoughts, something more than mere information or a passport to mere eking out one's life mechanically. Rabindra Nath Tagore (1861-1941), who was considered as an iconoclast in education, introduced freedom and joy in education. In the words of K.R. Srinivasa Iyengar:

> "He was poet, dramatist, actor, producer; he was musician and a painter; he was an educationist, a practical idealist who turned his dreams into reality at Shantiniketan; he was reformer, Philosopher, prophet; he was novelist and short story writer, and critic of life and literature, he even made occasional excursion into national politics, although he was essentially an internationalist; through his dramatic works without carrying for their stageability."[1] As Edward Thomson said, "His dramatic work is the vehicle of ideas rather than the expression of action."[2] Stressing upon the importance of joy and freedom in education Tagore attracts our attention towards harmony of the mind and the heart. And to attain this harmony, education should avoid all forms of parrot's training and artificiality. It must not be a forced or camouflaged product or outcome. For Tagore, Education is more than mere development. The aim of real education is to allow a learner to exercise joy and freedom and at the same time, evaluate and evolve in order to have the best of education. Tagore lost the world of joy as well as freedom in his own childhood as he was caged in the

four corners of the world and forced for the mechanical drill of repetition and cramming. It resulted in his escape from his schools.

As an ardent exponent of education for joy and freedom Tagore's remarks are based on his own experiences. I quote from one of Tagore's letters,

> Unfortunately, a boy in this country has a very little time at his disposal. He must learn a foreign language, pass several examinations, and qualify himself for a job in the shortest possible time, so, what can he do but cram up a few textbooks with breathless speed?...what I had particularly suffered in my childhood was to feel that the education that I had received was separated from life. That's why I do not advocate schools in the form of borrowed cages that treat the students' minds as captive birds, whose sole human value is judged according to the mechanical repetition of lessons prescribed by an educational dispensation foreign to the soil.[3]

The joy that one can derive from learning as a learner and teaching as a teacher is always an outcome of freedom that one can experience uninterruptedly. In fact freedom and joy make significant contributions to the right kind of education. Education should not be mere routine work of learning. He always allowed learners to learn more in living and thrilling contact with nature than from rot learning and cramming of ideals and thoughts from the old and decayed books. This was true in case of schools of the rural areas, where freedom to learn in joy was replaced by bookish education. As a mark of protest, he set up his own school—the Poet's School, Siksha-satra as he christens it—at Sriniketan, and wrote his aims in a letter to Leonard Knight Elmhrist—on December 19, 1937:

> You know how for a long time I have been cherishing my hope of establishing an ideal centre of education at Sriniketan—an ideal which is not curtailed to the strictest measure of a narrow village environment.... It is well-known that the education, which is prevalent in our country, is extremely meager in the spread of its area and barren in its quality.[4]

If there is no joy in the education it means that every kind of freedom is also absent *i.e.* freedom of thought, expression, creation and justification. Dull and mechanical learning is useless. Tagore elucidates how freedom and joy of the child in learning are continually neglected in our lifeless systems of education:

> Our system of education refuses to admit that children are children. Their educators do not know or they refuse to acknowledge that this childishness is Nature's own provision and that the child through its restless mind and movements should always come into touch with new facts and stumble upon new information.... I have a deep-rooted conviction that only through freedom man can attain his fullness of growth, and when we restrict that freedom it means that we have some purpose of our own which we impose on our children.[5]

I will relate this Tagorean concept of education with his play *Mukta Dhara*. The play has essentially a political theme but beneath the main plot Tagore reflects upon the problem of subordination of education to state monopoly. He wanted to give message that Education is a comprehensive process that eliminates all the ignorance of man, elevates him and frees him from the shackles of narrow mindedness to be able to evaluate things in relation to humanity as a whole. Tagore presents that knowledge must be utilized for the pleasure and prosperity of humanity. In the play *Mukta Dhara*, the School-master, with no name, appears once with a trail of well tutored boys, like parrots. He is to expose the evil of narrow nationalism with the misuse of education. The teacher, in order to have an increment in his salary, motivates the student to recite before the king about the glory of Utterakut.

The School-master does not want the boys to miss any opportunity. He trains the boys in such a way to spread the religions and racial prejudices. He is very strict with the students. He threatens to give them a taste of his came if they do not loudly shout 'Jai Raj Rajeshwar.' He also slaps a boy or two within his reach. Master assures the king that all these boys are being trained in such a way that they will be a terror one day to all the unhappy foreigners. An imperial regime gives rise to flatters as symbolized in the School-master of Utterakut, who is happy in training his students to be conscious of the superiority of their race and to treat all foreigners as inferior and fit only to be controlled and ruled and ordered about. He lacks intelligence, but being greedy he is more concerned with money rather than knowledge.

It reveals that such teachers are devoid of self-confidence and with their narrow views inculcate prejudices in the hearts of the students and spoil their cosmopolitan vision. However, as a realist Tagore realizes that the success of educational programmers is subordinate to bitter economic factor. Tagore recommends that to improve the Standard of education, due attention should be paid to the improvement of economic condition of teachers. The teacher in the play *Mukta Dhara* frankly confesses:

> Master: "Not for a moment do I forget what a great responsibility is ours. It is we school-masters who mould men—your ministers have merely to use them. Yet think what salary they get, compared with us." He further says "The boys are themselves our reward. Alas! but food is dear. Just think cow's ghee which used to be...."
>
> King Ranjit: "This School-master of yours has nothing in his head but ghee, cow's ghee."[6]

The scene is full of scorching wit and acid satire. Tagore holds to ridicule the real aim of a king regarding education by fully exposing it. The aim of the school-master to please the government and earn his bread is ridiculed and criticized. Tagore strongly believes it and that's why in his own educational institution he has introduced elements of freedom and joy as the most thrilling means of knowledge and wisdom. Freedom and joy can be taken as the heart and soul of Tagore's conception of an ideal education. He never favoured any sort of rigid or harsh discipline in the process of education. The atmosphere of rigid order and strict obedience enforces a cruel slavery, and is 'demoralizing' for children. H.B. Mukherjee has stated in this respect "Rough discipline, Tagore contended, is not only demoralizing for children; it degrades the teacher also. The mute subjection of his pupils adds to the autocratic propensities. Tagore had very strong words to use for repressive methods of dealing with children."[7]

This is just an evidence, through many letters, lectures and poetry Tagore made is clear that Education for expansion of freedom and love is; what the society earnestly looking forward to welcome the great vision of regeneration of humanity. He gave the message that under the favourable atmosphere the rich heritage of education for acceleration of freedom can be intensively nurtured. This finally we get the value-cocoon in Tagorean value system, experimented through diverse educational plans which incorporates the eight-fold quest.

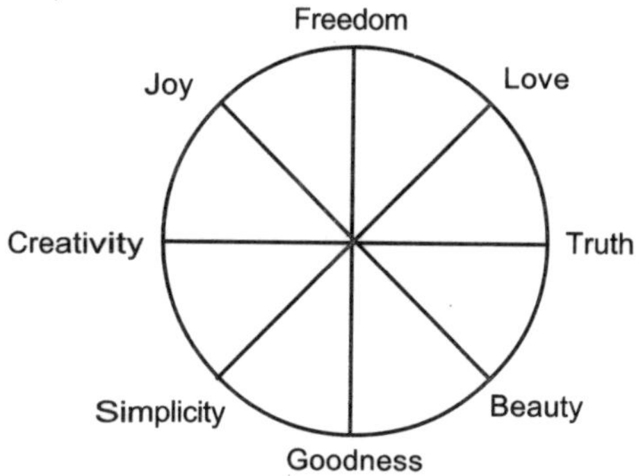

As element of joy being an inspirable education reminds us of mainly eight important objectives also. According to Mohit Chakravarti, they are as follows:

(a) For balanced growth and psychological development of a child, element of joy is essential to add in the system of education.

(b) To make education more meaningful, purposeful, living and innovative; joy and freedom should be harmonized in the process of learning as well as in teaching.

(c) Both the learner and the teacher should be free for the creative and critical inquisitiveness.

(d) Mechanical and humdrum, instructional strategies should be replaced by freedom because it allows nearness and cordiality.

(e) It is purely an Indian system of education.

(f) Education is the most dependable and accessible vehicle of training of mind and character.

(g) Essential skills of listening, speaking, reading and writing are produced in the most effective way if they are mixed with freedom and joy. Then only education will be highly interesting, thrilling and everlasting.

(h) Freedom should be such which can free oneself from the clutch of the educational system that tries to keep him imprisoned within the store-walls of lessons.

Tagore strongly believed that unless joy and freedom are the integral paw of the education, it is futile to, expect the rich dividends out of education. I conclude with four lines by Tagore written in Bangla in *Gitanjali* regarding his concept of Joy:

Let the light of joy of Man Eternal Amid all men
Be enkindled in my mind
Beyond the silent world of worldly grievances
Let me behold the blessed, form of the Eternal.[8]

References

1. K.R. Srinivasa Iyengar, *Indian Writing in English* (New Delhi: Sterling Publishers P. Ltd., 1987), 99.
2. Edward Thomson, *Rabindranath Tagore* (London: Oxford University Press, 1948), 47.
3. Tagore, Ranindranath, 'The Vicissitudes of Education' Towards Universal Man, Asia Publishing House, 1961, 1.
4. Tagore, Rabindranath, Letter to L.K. Elmhist quoted in Rabindranathen Chintaiagat: Sikshrchinte, Satyendranath Roy, G. Ranthaly, P. Ltd., Calcutta 1982, 324-25.
5. Tagore, Rabindranath, 'The School Master: The Modern Review,' Calcutta, October 1924, 369-72.
6. Mukherjee, H.B., *Education for Fullness*, Asia Publishing House, Bombay, 1962; 370.
7. Tagore, Rabindranath, "Muktadhara": Tandon Neeru (A critical study of Tagore's *Muktadhara*: Mitra Publication, Kanpur), 86-87.
8. Tagore, Rabindranath, *Gitanjali*.

TAGORE'S *CHITRA*: AN EPITOME OF LOVE, TRUTH AND BEAUTY

19

Reshu Shukla

Rabindranath Tagore's plays are basically expressions of the soul's quest for beauty and truth. A close study of his plays reveals that Tagore probed deep into the mind of woman and presented a wide range of female characters. He drew the attention of his readers on numerous cases of social injustice especially to woman. Besides this, he placed before the whole world the ideal to self-reliant in Indian woman fighting not for their own rights and desires but also for those of the subjugated nationality and downtrodden humanity. By his well-known play *Chitra* he has presented a very sensible and revolutionary picture of a common woman.

Rabindranath Tagore's *Chitra* is a dramatic sermon on the theme of true love. This lyrical drama, written in 1913, the year when Tagore received the Nobel Prize; is based on the story of the 'Mahabharta.' Chitra is the first clear exposition of feminism in India by Tagore. This play is a work of supreme art, a dream of flawless beauty in an awakened state. Tagore's conception of human love finds a beautiful expression in Chitra.

Chitra is the daughter of the King Manipur. She is brought up as a boy by her parents. She acquires perfection in handling bow and arrow and faithfully discharges her duty towards the state like a Kshatriya King and safeguards the interests of her people. Tagore's Chitra is an epitome of youth, love and romance. Though she is a woman, but very well aware of her responsibilities towards her state. She gets exceptional physical power but is deprived of all feminine sensibilities and attractions that may impress a man. She confesses that she can bend the bow 'but does not know' cupids archery 'and the play of eyes.' During his exile, Arjuna, the Pandava prince, meets Chitra. Splendour of his masculine personality stimulates her suppressed feminine sensibility. She says:

> Then for the first time in my life.
> I felt myself a woman and know
> that a man was before me.[1]

She feels vacuum within and craves for physical beauty to capture the heart of Arjuna and discards all her boy-like garments and manners. After being spurned by Arjuna, she forms a resolve to win Arjuna's love by employing unfair means, and gets success in generating intense infatuation in his heart. But with an extra-ordinary power of self-analysis she realized that she was loved by Arjuna not for her innate qualities, but for her borrowed beauty. In the end true love blazes forth from the ashes of the false love which has existed till now. The play depicts the evolution of human love from the physical to the spiritual one.

Tagore's *Chitra* is like Kalidas's *Shakuntala*, epitome of youth, love and romance. Chitra is an unself-conscious girl, wearing a boy's attire. She has been portrayed by Tagore as a bare simplicity of truth. To realize her ambition she reveals her agony and makes a declaration:

> I am not the woman who nourishes her despair in lonely silence, feeding it with nightly tears and covering it with the daily patient smile, a widow from her birth. The flower of my desire shall never drop into the dust before it has ripened to fruit.[2]

Chitra is a significant fusion of the two kinds of woman characters—the emotional and the tranquilling type. Chitra is not learned archery, growing from innocent girlhood to the mellowness of motherhood; which can be traced from drawn to reality and the transition from the fire of flowery spring to the mellow fruitfulness of Autumn. She advances from the paradise of sensual rapture to the ecstasy of illumination and the sustaining delight of wisdom.

The feminine charm she has acquired after the experience makes her,

> The Mother, throned on the fullness of golden Autumn, she who in the harnest time brings, straying hearts to the smile sweet as tears, the beauty deep as the sex of silence, brings them to the temple of the unknown, at the holy opulence of Life and Death.[3]

Arjuna accepts her in bliss when she casts on him a tranquilling spell,

> Beloved, My life is full.[4]

Rabindranath Tagore's conception of human love finds a beautiful expression in Chitra. We get in Chitra's personality the first clear exposition of feminism in India, whose representation she is. The play promotes the very concept of equality of women even in the field specially reserved for men; Chitra is not the woman who arouses her despair in lonely silence, she is no goddess to be worshipped, nor yet the object of common pity to be brushed aside like a moth with indifference. She has certainly lost one paradise but she has gained another instead, which is the real paradise where woman holds undisputed sovereignty as devoted wife and mother.

By the character of Chitra, Tagore has forcefully portrayed the picture of modern Indian woman, promoting the higher spiritual and psychological sensibilities. On the one hand Chitra is a very promising princess and bears all the responsibilities towards kingdom on the other hand she is a devoted beloved of Arjuna, and becomes the victim of love and emotions. Arjuna thinks of her as a goddess of victory and says:

> like a watchful lioness she protects the litter at her dugs with a fierce love. Woman's arms though adorned with nought, but unfettered strength, are beautiful! My heart is restless, fair one, like a serpent, reviving from his long winter's sleep. Come, let us both race on swift horses by side, like twin orbs of light sweeping through space.[5]

Chitra is a bold, courageous, daring, determined and moreover she is full of the feeling of dedication and devotion towards her duties. She has all the capabilities, which a king should have. If she lacks in something that is womanly grace, tenderness and over all physical charm.

By Chitra Tagore has revealed two aspects of woman the first one is strongest enough to win the biggest battle of the world and the other one that easily gets shattered by one flow of emotion. She is a complete personality of a woman, who not only has commendable patience, sacrifice and dedication but also is ready to face any situation at the cost of fulfilling her ambitions and desires. Tagore has beautifully symbolized her as a great mental conflict on the one hand, and the symbol of strength and determination on the other. Chitra has a tender heart within her strong body, she wilfully changes her personality for the sake of love but also let not die her existence. Chitra suffered a great mental conflict while presenting her false endeavour before Arjuna and says:

> My body has become my own rival. It is my hateful task to deck her everyday, to send her to my beloved and see her caressed by him.[6]

This attitude reveals the reality about the very nature of the woman, that for sake of love and true relationship she can do any thing up to any extent and can sacrifice her life too. But when the matter comes on her existence she is ready to loose the most precious thing of her life. She says:

> I will reveal my true self to him, a nobler thing than this disguise. If he rejects it, if he spurn me and break my heart; I will bear even that in silence.[7]

Though she gets success in winning the heart of Arjuna by her borrowed sublime grace but she fails before her own self. Chitra very soon realizes the misdeed she has done and wants to deprive herself from that falsehood which unfortunately becomes the base of that pious feeling. She is ready to come out of her illusive face and wants her true self loved by Arjuna which is capable enough to participate in his every brave action. She says to Arjuna:

> If you deign to keep me by your side, in the path of danger and daring, if you allow me to share the great duties of your life then you will know my true self.[8]

This is what the new feminist movement in India stands for as it was heralded by Tagore and these words of Chitra are undoubtedly a great source of inspiration to the young educated females of India in twentieth century.

Though Chitra is not gifted by the tenderness of flowers but has challenging courage like great warriors, may her eyes are not attractive but everybody likes to see bow in her hand. Men may not get attracted towards her physical charm but brave salute her.

The play is a journey from the physical attraction to the spiritual love and Chitra acts as a bridge between two feelings. Though she gets infatuated towards the heroic splendour of Arjuna but when Arjuna offers his love to Chitra and is ready to break his vow of celibacy for the sake of her physical charm which she got from the god for winning the love of Arjuna. Chitra is not thrilled with joy, the real sense of woman becomes gradually stronger and she says:

> Whom do you seek in these dark eyes, in these milk-white arms, if you are ready to pay for her the price of your probity? Not my true self, I know. Surely this cannot be loved, this is not man's highest homage to woman! Alas, that this frail disguise, the body, should make one blind to the light of deathless spirit! Yes, now indeed, I know, Arjuna, the fame of your heroic manhood is falls.[9]

Chitra candidly confesses what she is in actuality. She lights from the world of dreams, poetry and romance woven around her to the world of reality, where by the delicate play things of transient youth which she had clocked around her self, now leave her. Arjuna never seems to comprehend her as he considers her to be a goddess hidden within a golden icon on account of which he cannot touch her and pay her his homage in return for her priceless gifts. She advances with a false front towards Arjuna, her lover. But shortly later, the time arrives when she throws off her ornaments and veils, and stands clothed in unsheathed dignity.

Chitra is fully conscious that her procured beauty would shortly vanish, as the petals fall from an overblown flower, the only moment of her sweet union would slip from her, leaving her ashamed of her exposed poverty, which she will spend weeping day and night. It is impossible for her to keep her disguise and she prefers to accept hard truth sooner then the false happiness.

Now the illusion is shattered and Chitra, the playmate of Arjuna's night, appears as the help mate of the day showing her true self. Chitra says:

> The gift that I proudly bring you is the heart of a woman. Here have all pains and joys gathered, the hopes and fears and shames of a daughter of the dust. Here love springs up struggling towards immortal life. Herein lies an imperfection, which yet is noble and grand. If the flower-service is finished, my master, accept this as your servant for the days to come![10]

Thus before parting from Chitra, Arjuna accepts her in bliss when she casts on him a tranquilizing spell. Chitra becomes all the more beautiful because she has known love, and because she is now a prospective mother.

Tagore has very well succeeded in creating women in her complete endeavour, for him woman in true sense is the most strong and the most tender creation of God. Women are the enthroned queens of the house full of self-respect and self-consideration, showing various moods. Chitra's words of surrender to Arjuna best sum up Tagore's attitude to women. Chitra boldly admits:

> I am Chitra no goddess to be worshipped, or yet the object of common pity to be brushed aside like a moth with indifference.[11]

Through Chitra, as an epitome of love, truth and beauty, Tagore brings home to us the simple truth of life that beauty and youth, although they may be transient, are yet a part of our experience.

References

1. R.N. Tagore, *Chitra*, A play in one act. Prakash Book Depot, Bara Bazar, Bareily-243003, 6.
2. *Ibid.*, 8.
3. *Ibid.*
4. *Ibid.* 24.
5. *Ibid.*, 22.
6. *Ibid.*, 14.
7. *Ibid.*, 15.
8. *Ibid.*, 24.
9. *Ibid.*, 11.
10. *Ibid.*, 24.
11. *Ibid.*, 24.

VIJAY TENDULKAR: A CRITICAL SURVEY OF HIS DRAMATIC WORLD

20

Anshul Chandra

Vijay Tendulkar (b. 1928) is a leading contemporary Indian playwright. He is also known as screen and television writer, literary essayist, political journalist and social commentator. In the realm of drama he has been the most influential dramatist and theatre personality in Marathi. He is a man of radical and progressive views. He is the author of thirty full-length plays and twenty-three one act plays, several of which have become classics of modern India theatre. His *Silence! the Court is in Session* earned him a place among leading Indian playwrights in late sixties while his *Ghasiram Kotwal* won him international fame in the mid-seventies.

Vijay Tendulkar's first major play *Manus Navache Bet* (An Island Called Man, 1955) gave expression to the tormenting solitude and alienation of a modern individual in an urbane industrialized society. *Manus Navache Bet* was followed by a number of plays like *Madhlya Bhinti* (The Walls Between, 1950), *Chimnicha Ghar Hota Menacha* (Nest of Wax, 1950), *Mee Jinklo Mee Harlo* (I Won, I Lost, 1963), *Kavlanchi Shala* (School for Crows, 1963) and *Sari Ga Sari* (Rain, O Rain, 1964). In all these plays Vijay Tendulkar is concerned with the middle class individual set against the backdrop of a hostile society. He presents modern man in all his complexities. For Vijay Tendulkar the primary compulsion is and has always been humanistic. Man's fight for survival, the varied moralities by which people live, the social position of women, the covert or overt violence in human being, these are his abiding concerns. They appear in his plays in different forms. *Shantala!*

Court Chalu Ahe (Silence! The Court is in Session, 1967) was his first play in which he marked out as a rebel against the established values of fundamentally orthodox society. This play combines social criticism with the tragedy of an individual victimized by society.

His play *Dambadwipcha Mukabala* (Encounter in Umbugland) is completely different from his previous play. *Dambadwipcha Mukabala* is one of his first political plays. The political satire of this play exposes the secrets of politics that are designed to reach positions of authority.

Ghasiram Kotwal (1972) is also a political play. This play is a musical combining Marathi folk performance styles and contemporary theatrical techniques. *Ghasiram Kotwal* is one of the longest running plays in the world with over six thousand performance in India and abroad. This play is set in a historical background and every detail of dress, gesture and movement described is very realistic. It focuses on the power games that men engage in and the corruption, violence and sensuality in which they indulge in the process.

All of Vijay Tendulkar's plays concentrate on different aspect of the human character and complexity of human relationship. His greatest quality is to simultaneously involve and distance himself from his works. All of his works are clearly distinct from each other. He considers himself a writer of plays and film scripts on a wide variety of subjects, not a closet philosopher or a sociologist who has missed his vocation. Over the last few decades, he has scanned the life-world of contemporary Indian in order to identify the sources and nature of the violence that has come to pattern it. Even when violence is not ostensibly his theme, it casts it shadow on his characters. It is unjust to read his entire work as a commentary on human violence.

Vijay Tendulkar's perspective on violence is bifocal. In his work *Gidhade* (The Vultures, 1971), violence tends to become an end in itself. It is the easiest way left for many ordinary citizens to cope with their fractured selves and problems of living. No longer does violence come from ideology, faith or even self-interest. On the contrary it seeks outlet through ideology, faith and perceived self-interest and latches on to these "causes" to find public expression and legitimacy. In this paradoxical world, violence is prior to its causes. *Gidhade* is based on sex, violence and evil. According to Girish Karnad "the staging of *Gidhade* could be compared to the blasting of a bomb in an otherwise complacent marketplace. Publication of *Gidhade,* has made him one of most distinguished social theorists of violence in the country. Vijay Tendulkar has said that *Gidhade* was born out of a personal crisis in his life. It shows the degeneration of a family with compassion and cruelty. *Gidhade* is an outstanding example of Vijay Tendulkar's modernity.

Sakharam Binder is Tendulkar's most intensely naturalistic play. According to critics, "for many decades no play has created such a sensation in the theatre world of Maharashtra as Vijay Tendulkar's Marathi play *Sakharam Binder.* It explores the complication of human nature and the manifestation of physical lust and violence in a human being. After production of *Sakharam Binder* Tendulkar was accused of deliberately choosing sensational themes to get cheap publicity. He says, "Every play is not for everybody," "A play is a work of art when it reveals its theme and essence exclusively through its mode attendant detailing rather than through statement and speech." *Sakharam Binder* fulfils these criteria and is therefore an artistic play.

Kanyadaan (Daughters Gifted Away, 1983) is also indicative of Tendulkar's variations in his dramatic creations. In this play he portrayed a Dalit writer as a drunkard, wife beater, manipulator and blackmailer. This is not expected of a writer whose public life spoke of a strong liberal humanist ideology. *Kanyadaan* is a good play with which to enter the trouble area of public and critical response to Tendulkar's play.

Vijay Tendulkar writes his plays with so much theatrical craft that a good production is assured by simply following his stage directions. According to Vikram Gokhale:

> There is an invisible director in Tendulkar who keeps making a variety of suggestions to the adventurous playwright in him from time to time. Once in a while the sensitive spectator and the ruthless critic in him also prick and prod the playwright. That is why the playwright walks along the straight path of truth to the predetermined end, strewing brackets as he proceeds, before, between or after dialogues, filling them with the most valuable stage directions. The guidance they provide to the director, actor and reader is of great help. It is my belief that even a moderately intelligent director or actor would do a good job of a Tendulkar play the more gifted of course would reap immense success.[1]

Vijay Tendulkar has created memorable male and female characters. He explores the position of women in contemporary Indian society through his female characters. It is his women, who help to reveal his social conscience on account of their position in society. As characters Tendulkar's women are among the most convincing in Indian theatre. He depicts women as being equal underneath their socio-economic class.

Kamala (1981) is a tropical drama inspired by a real life incident. Like most of his sympathetic women characters Kamala does not have the spirit to rebel against her present condition. As the centre of the play is a self-seeking journalist, Jaisingh Jadav, who has bought Kamala for Rs. 250 at an auction is a flesh market. He wants to present her at a surprises press conference to prove that such things still happen in modern, democratic India. Using this incident in his drama, Tendulkar raises certain cardinal questions regarding the value system of a modern success-oriented generation who are ready to sacrifice human values even in the name of humanity itself.

In most of his plays, Vijay Tendulkar presents women in pairs. They are quite different from each other. He portrays them as loyal, docile, religious, hardworking, self-effacing and tender-hearted, the other type of woman is more selfish, wily, vicious and assertive. Even then they resemble each other in the ultimate truth of being commanded by men, for their pleasure and under their laws.

In *Shantala! Court Chalu Ahe,* Leela Benare is young, single, unconventional, full of laughter and pride. Mrs. Kashikar on the other hand is middle aged, married, a housewife and disapproving of "free" woman like Leela Benare. She is Childless. Mrs. Kashikar thinks that it is an automatic right of a man to insults and snubs a woman because of being a man and husband. She does not oppose her insults and still seen Mr. Kashikar as a caring husband because he has bought a string of flower for her hair, a token of romance not love.

Leela Benare on the other hand ignores social norms and dictates. She is competing for equality with men in their own world. In her views, men must prove themselves before they can command her respect. She has an illicit love affair with a married man and gets pregnant but he does not have the strength to own his child. At last she becomes prey to the hypocrisy and double standard of our society.

In *Gidhade* Manik and Rama are bolder contrasts. Rama is sensitive, naturally kind and good hearted. Her illicit relationship with her half-brother-in-law, Rajininath is the only gray shade of her life. Manik is one of the vultures; she is the classic "slut" and hops from one bed to another. The contrast between Manik and Rama is black and white. Manik is only a female vulture who will ultimately get some compassion. Her two brothers force her to abort her baby and kick her unborn child. At last her dead father's spirits, evil even in death, laughing at her fate. *Gidhade* depicts how the mutual hatred among the members of the family, degenerates it.

Laxmi and Champa in *Sakharam Binder* are another pair of women who share a common condition having contrast characters. Laxmi is an ideal Indian woman and a good wife but turns out to be wily and vicious when her survival is threatened by Champa. Champa on the other hand is like the socially despised temptress. It is through Champa that Tendulkar shows how deep-rooted women's exploitation in society is. It is Champa who convinces Sakharam to give shelter to Laxmi because she is confident of her own sexual attractions. These women satisfy the domestic and physical needs of Sakharam.

Laxmi develops a sexual relationship with Shinde and Champa develops sexual relationship with Daud Miyan. It is Laxmi who uses this opportunity to take revenge because her moral sense is outraged by Champa's illicit relationship.

In *Kamala,* Sarita and Kamala are contrast to each other. Sarita is educated and self-assured while Kamala is illiterate village woman. Sarita is the wife of Jadav and is childless. It is illiterate Kamala who understands the man-woman relationship and says to Sarita:

> Madam, can I say something if it won't upset you? The owner has bought you and he has bought me. He's shelled out big money for two women, no?... so we must stay together here, like two sisters. We'll keep the owner happy....

Once Sarita sees herself, as a slave and decided to leave her husband but when Jadav is betrayed by his editor, she gives him moral support. This shows a compassionate human being in her.

In his plays Tendulkar describes the basic and essential complexity of human nature, which is neither black nor white but varying shades of gray. He has portrayed his characters with utmost. His all characters are a combination of good and evil. He depicts his male characters by class and social position. His male characters come from the middle class and face the problem of achievement in the outside world.

In most of his works he deals with different aspect of the human character. In an interview he said, "The history of human culture has taken very complex twists and turns. Yet, even today, my inspirational strength lies in the hope with which I look forward to tomorrow. I have consistently depicted the indomitability and grit of the human spirit in my writings. But I have never allowed that to lead me into drawing unreal, comforting conclusions.[2]

This statement explains his themes with social and aesthetic ideas of Tendulkar's playwriting. Exploration of woman relationship, social-individual tensions of the society, alienation of the modern individual to contemporary politics are the themes of his plays. None of his creations are ever simplistic—like him they too give new meanings to one's understandings. His sense of humour and intense compassion are two other hallmarks of his creative self. He continues to experiment and explore the potentials of the dramatic genre—his primary area of creation.

Notes

1. Natak Ani Mee—selected writings on theatre, Vijay Tendulkar, Dimple Publication, Thane, 1997, "Mazha Natya Shikshan" (My Theatre Education), 96-97.
2. Natak Ani Mee, Vijay Tendulkar, Dimple Publication, Thane, 1997, Interview with Shirish Pai, Priya Tendulkar, 188.

21 MAN-WOMAN RELATIONSHIP IN THE "SAKHARAM BINDER"

Indulekha Roy Burman

Contemporary Indian Drama offers us a wide spectrum of life. Most of the playwrights have shown a deep penchant for the study of man as a prisoner of society, as a child of his own milieu. The interplay between man and society and man and woman position in the present drama. The prominent progenitors of contemporary Indian Drama include Girish Karnad, Vijay Tendulkar, Mahesh Dattani, Badal Sircar, Mohan Rakesh and so on.

Vijay Tendulkar is perhaps the most prolific and controversial among the post-Independence Indian playwrights. An icon of India's vernacular Marathi theatre and the doyen of the avant-garde Indian Theatrical Movement of the modern era, Tendulkar's plays are at once disturbing, moving and provocative. They reflect a magical combination of currency, topicality and timelessness. The dramatist's portrayal of man-woman relationship is charged with a sensitive yet dispassionate study of human nature. It is a kind of fierce naturalism that banishes all the artist-made artificiality or gaudiness of imagination from the domain of the drama. It is his fanatic passion for the 'real' that makes him present life in the 'raw' sans any sugar coating.

Each of Tendulkar's plays is an enigma by itself that sensitizes the readers or the audience to all the beastly as well as redeeming aspects of man-woman relationship. He is poignantly alert to the vulgar, the pervert and the violent to which man has shown a natural proclivity. The astonishing range of his plays, be it the victimization of the individual by a hyporcritical society in "Silence! the Court is in Session," sexual degeneration and moral collapse of a family in "The Vultures," ruthlessness of media and marriage as a farcical institution in "Kamala" the sheer bawdiness and bloodyness in "Sakharam Binder," the issue of class conflict in "Kanyadaan" or the concept of romantic love with both of its homosexual and heterosexual aspects in "A Friend's Story"— shows a shocking but genuine complexity of human relationships and is bereft of any moralizing that gives them a very open-ended feel.

"Sakharam Binder" is a fascinating study of the relationship between man and woman. It dissects the morbid, squalid aspects of human life against a bizarre backdrop of Plebeian society. Here, Tendulkar's love for the macabre and the obsession with sex and violence as an integral part of human nature and relationships receive a vitriolic expression. The brutal objectivity and crudity with which he depicts the triangular relationship between Sakharam and his two mistresses, Laxmi and Champa, sometimes borders on a sort of revelry into the Philistinism in literature. The eponymous hero abhors marriage as an institution and believes in contractual cohabitation without rites. His passion is to bring to his den wives deserted by their husbands or who have walked out on them. What Sakharam the patron of 'symbiotic' polygamy, demands from his mistresses, is absolute submission along with domestic comfort and physical gratification. The wretched women are turned into his slaves in his kitchen as well as in his bed. They are also promptly dismissed from his haven on the slightest offence.

Sakharam's life receives a big jolt after the intrusion of his seventh and eighth women, Laxmi and Champa respectively, into his household. These two women represent two polarities of feminine response towards this sensual patriarch. Laxmi oozes the eternal 'oomph' of a traditional Indian woman with her god-fearing religious, docile nature and her unflinching devotion towards her husband, no matter how great a tyrant he is. When she is thrown out of her house by her husband on her failure to give birth to a child and is rescued by Sakharam, she accepts the vicissitudes of life without any protest. She clutches Sakharam as her only option to survive and begins to worship her 'Saviour.' She demonstrates the patterns of thinking instilled in women by the patriarchal tradition. But Champa is a boiling couldron of fierce revolt that guts down all the men around her, irrespective of her protector or annihilator. She is a woman who has walked on her alcoholic husband as a strong rebuff to his cruelty perpetrated upon her. In her, Tendulkar points out that marriage is an institution in which sexual relationship for a woman is possible only if the self is forgotten in the stupor of alcohol, pleasure is possible only through inflicting pain on the others and 'self-awareness' is nothing but the mute and moron-like acceptance of inhuman subordination or supremacy. The wild, wayward, vivacious and defiant Champa's final surrender to Sakharam, after considerable resistance, signifies a kind of 'compromise' or 'payment' for what she has been provided by him—food, clothe and shelter.

Champa and Shinde, her former husband, once again bring out the sordid aspect of a degenerated relationship. The effeminate sex sick pervert Shinde, who is desperately in search of his run-away bride Champa, talks of her, like a puerile man, as if she is a cow or a buffalo (the size of her buttocks and breasts etc.). And Champa, having brushed aside the bitter fact that this man is her husband, abuses her as a 'corpse' and a 'ninny.' Dawood, Sakharam's friend sums up their connubial status brilliantly, "So, this is the bird's cage.... If the bird comes, its cage is bound to follow" (165). Marriage puts the woman, the bird, in cage symbolised by her husband. Even if the bird flies, the cage chases her. There is no 'riddance.'

However, the play is set on motion when Sakharam, Champa and Laxmi embark upon a trilateral symbiotic relationship under the initiative of Champa who, confident of her 'physical superiority to Laxmi's' arranges for the latter's permanent lodging in her household. With a cool business-like attitude, that is reminiscent of Sakharam's, Champa confers upon Laxmi all the menial arduous tasks of the household and herself takes the charge of quenching Sakharam's unabashed sexual hunger. It is curious to note, how Sakharam is gradually being usurped from his own position as a decision-maker. But while the two women somehow adjust with the new set-up, Sakharam the veteran womanizer, now feels too fettered to indulge in his lust for Champa as freely with Laxmi around. As he secretly writhes under the agony of a growing sense of impotence, Champa, probably cured of frigidity, initiates a clandestine affair with Dawood and proffers to him a share of her animal appetite, the 'official proprietor' of which is Sakharam. Laxmi, on the other hand, while developing a secret asexual relationship with Shinde, Champa's wretched husband, senses a potent enemy in the form of Champa. When Laxmi finds Champa and Dawood in an objectionable condition, her sense of morality gets immediately beefed up against Champa's fornication. In Laxmi we find a queer amalgamation of a genuine fellow-feeling for the opposite sex *viz.*, Sakharam, Shinde and a virtual non-understanding of the same sex, the latter partially being due to her urge for survival in an unequal triangular relationship. She cannot bear the misery of Shinde and accept the betrayal committed against Sakharam by Champa. But she remains surprisingly blind to Champa's generosity towards her and the fact that Champa herself once used to be tortured by her husband.

Laxmi's discovery of Champa's incest with Dawood not only gives her a feeling of victory but also serves as a trump card that she can play at the vital moment. To Champa, on the other hand, Sakharam has turned a 'vegetable' who cannot 'ignite' her anymore. She finds in Dawood a 'nice' substitute, rather a more calm humane and circumspect surrogate lover. Sakharam, in the meanwhile, has reached a point of exasperation after a spell of impotence he has been experiencing in his relationship with Champa who has started resisting his sexual advances. So, in order to reach a conclusion a maddened Sakharam decides to uproot the 'weed' Laxmi who has eaten up his pleasure garden. When Laxmi is about to be kicked out of the house, she blurts out, half-terrorized by Sakharam, Champa's infidelity. The balance tilts immediately. In his impotent and chaotic mental state, Sakharam throttles Champa to death, with Laxmi being a willing accomplice. After the murder, the play takes a gruesome turn when an ecstatic, hysterical Laxmi viciously eggs on the murderer to cover up the killing of Champa, her rival in the triangular relationship. It is a pity that Laxmi who accepts and upholds patriarchal value system, loathes Champa for betraying her husband Sakharam and sees her death as a divine retribution. Such blind belief in an oppressive system appears even more stifling; than Champa's gross fornication and vulgarity.

The play ends with Sakharam's pride shattered. The bitter critic of marriage as an institution is proved, at the end, to be a puny male chauvinist. Though he detested the tyrannical husbands he himself is no better than them. He made sarcastic remarks about the wives' loyalty to their despotic husbands but he himself demands utmost obedience from his mistresses. He represents the double standards of patriarchy. By 'helping' the women in distress, this pseudo-misogynist indirectly subjected them to a kind of prostitution. The myth of his working class secularism is exploded as the sexual jealousy in him wells up only when Champa shares her bed with Dawood, a Muslim. The metamorphosis of Laxmi, within the very territory of the patriarchal framework, from a meek to a murderous lady who performs religious rites and homicide with considerable aplomb, deflates the ego-centric male-power in the play. It seems that the sex-oriented patriarch gives way to a meticulous and conservative matriarch (who has ironically internalized oppression perpetrated by patriarchy) to rule his little 'philanthropic,' polygamous monarchy.

Suggested Readings

Vijay Tendulkar, *Sakharam Binder*, Trans. Kumad Mehta and Shanta Gokhale; Vijay Tendulkar: *Five Plays*, New Delhi: Oxford University Press, 1992.

M. Sarat Babu, *Indian Drama Today: A Study in the Theme of Cultural Deformity*, Prestige Books, New Delhi.

Sudhakar Pandey and Freya Taraporewala (ed.), *Contemporary Indian Drama*, Prestige Books, New Delhi.

Maya Pandit, *Representation of Family in Modern Marathi Plays*, Theatre India, Nov. 2000.

Catherina Thankamma, *The Women Patriarchy Created*, Theatre India, Nov. 2000.

INDIAN ENGLISH WOMEN PLAYWRIGHTS

22

Anjana Trivedi

Indian English Drama has shot into prominence quite recently. It has made a fresh ground both technically and thematically; enabling the audience to share a new experience not only of the external world but also of the internal world of psyche. It has become a composite art involving the mind of the dramatist, action of the protagonists and the reaction of the audience. Apart from the substantial contributions rendered in this field by the noted dramatists like Girish Karnad, Nissim Ezekiel, and Mahesh Duttani, some minor Indian English women playwrights have also published their plays in the last two decades of the twentieth century.

Mahasweta Devi, the Bengali writer was born on the 14th January, 1926 in the city of Dacca, in East Bengal, now known as Bangladesh. Later on her family moved to West Bengal. She was deeply influenced by her early association with Gananatya, a group who aimed to bring social and political theatre to rural villages in Bengal in the 1930's and 1940s.

Mahasweta Devi studied in Shantiniketan and received Master's Degree in English Literature from Calcutta University. She began working as a teacher and journalist. She started writing in 1939 and her first writing was published in a Bengali Magazine, "Rang Mashaal." Her first book "Jhansir Rani" was published in 1956. This marked the beginning of her prolific literary career. She has written 42 novels, a number of articles, reportage and a collection of plays. She has been a regular contributor to several literary magazines such as

'Bortika,' a journal dedicated to the cause of the oppressed communities within India. In 1948 she retired from her job as an English Lecturer at a Calcutta University to concentrate more on her writings. More than two hundred books, written by Mahasweta Devi, have been published. Though basically she is a Bengali writer, yet her works are translated not only into the languages spoken in India but in foreign languages like English, French and Japanese etc. also. She has crossed the bounds of time and place and today she is recognized as a writer of international repute.

The most recurrent theme of Devi's works surrounds the untouchables for their basic human rights. All her plays express the playwright's deep concern for the untouchables who are denied their fundamental rights. In her writings, we find the portrayal of the anguish and agony of the down-trodden, Societal and legal violations of human rights to Dalits and tribals, women and children. The main issue troubling her mind is the livelihood (Roti) of the poor. Her answer to any social problem is: "Roti is the greatest controller. No political power is as strong as Roti and Rice." The 'marginalized man' of the society is at the centre of all the writings of Mahasweta Devi.

The play "Aajir" is the story of a slave held so by a bond signed by an ancestor a slavery that denies him the right to love and to live freely. The agony and anguish and the heart-felt problems are apparent through a dialogue by Paatan, who realizes that his fate is doomed as long as the bond exists. "The play portrays how the down-trodden have been treated like slaves, denied human dignity in the name of a bond which had already turn to dust; their struggle against human violations and ultimate freedom, a cause for which Mahasweta Devi has been fighting for the past fifty years or so."[1]

In another important play "Water," Devi depicts how the tribal people in a rural area in West Bengal have been denied basic right to water by the upper caste feudal lords, represented by Santosh Pujary who collects money for relief just to misuse it for his vested interest. "It is women who suffer most due to the non-availability of water.... Having denied the opportunity to collect water from public well during day time, they try to steal water during night time but the landlord lets his dogs loose on them. The non-availability of drinking water poses threat to their very survival and hence all the women join in singing praying to their gods for water:

Give us water!
Water! Water! Water!"[2]

Mahasweta Devi through this play has exposed all kinds of discrimination, exploitation and atrocities done to the tribals/Dalits. The Naxalite movement of the late 1960's and early 1970's were also important influence in her work. This leftist militant movement which started in the Naxalbari region of West Bengal, began as a rural revolt of landless workers and tribal people against landlords and moneylenders. Devi's "Hajar Chaurashi Ma" (Mother of 1084) is the story of an upper middle class woman whose world is forever changed when her son is killed for his Naxalite belief. This work has been translated into Hindi language and popularized as a movie called "Hazar Chaurasi Ki Ma" directed by Govind Nihalani. In fact her plays have championed the cause of human rights to Dalits/tribals. Such concerns can be seen in works such as 'Aranyer Adhikar' (Rights of the Forest) published in 1977, based on the life of Birsa Munda; a tribal freedom fighter. She has donated the prize money both from the Jnanpath and Magasaysay awards to tribal communities and continues to use her work to further the position of these groups in India.

Mahasweta Devi believes that a creative writer should have a social conscience, a duty towards society. In response to the question, "What would you like to do for the rest of your life?" in a 1998 interview Devi replied, "Fight for the tribals, down-trodden, unprivileged and write creatively if and when I find the time."

Equally important name among Indian English Women dramatists is Uma Parameswaran.

Uma Parameswaran, a poet, play-wright, short story writer, was born in Madras and grew up in Jabalpur. She graduated from Jabalpur University and completed her post-graduation in English and diploma in Journalism from Nagpur University. She was a Fulbright Scholar and received an M.A. in Creative Writing (Indiana University) and a Ph.D. in English (Michigan State University, 1972). Her areas of research are English Romantic, Post Colonial literatures, Women's Literature and South Asian Canadian Literature. Her teaching areas are Post-Colonial Literature, Women's Literature and creative writing. At present she is a professor of English at the University of Winnipeg and holds the prestigious position as a Regional Representative, National Council of the Writers' Union of Canada.

Uma Parmeswaran started her literary career as a newspaper reporter in India. She has written plays that were published in Toronto and India. She has to her credit the authorship and editorship of ten scholarly books dealing with post-colonial literature and feminism. A number of her articles and essays have published in many renowned journals. She has also been active in the Writers Union of Canada, serving on the National Council in various capacities throughout the 1990's. In order to introduce various aspects of Indian culture not only to the Indo-Canadian youth of Winnipeg, but also to the total community at large, she has founded PALI—Performing Arts and Literatures of India. After a gap of several years PALI sponsored a unique music concert in Sept. 1997 at the University of Winnipeg, featuring 3 artists—an accomplished vocalist, Ravi Srinivasan, accompanied on the violin by Jayshankar Balan and on the mridangam by Desikan Narayanan—all role models of positive diasporic culture.

Uma Parameswaran has been taking keen interest to bring Indian culture and heritage to the children of Winnipeg for the last twenty-five years. With this mission she organized the first formal dance training in 1978 in Winnipeg.

Uma Parameswaran, while staying in Indian during 1960's wrote 'Sons Must Die,' a play based on the theme of the partition of 1947. Soon after that a series of renowned plays by her followed: 'Meera in 1971,' 'Sita's Promise' in 1981, 'Dear Didi,' 'My Sister,' in 1989, 'Rootless but green are the

Boulevard Trees,' in 1998. All these plays collected into 'Sons must Die and other Plays' and published in 1998 as a part of South Asian Canadian Literature Series (SACLIT), of which Uma Parameswaran is the general editor.

'Sons Must Die' exposes the experiences of three women in 1947 India. The plot structure, technique and style of the play depicts Uma Parameswaran's interest in Greek tragedies.

Pacifistic and prophetic in tone, the play, "Sons Must Die" depicts the horrors of war and is set in the backdrop of Kashmir (Indo-Pak war of 1947-48). Here three women from different parts of India; a Tamil Brahmin, wrapped in conjeevaram silk, Zohra begum a Muslim mother wearing a Salwar Kameez suit with gold embroidery on the blue velvet and Prem Behn, a Punjabi mother all meet at Kashmir in search of their sons. All these three mothers have lost their sons who were at the battlefield fighting for Kashmir.

Meenakshi says:

> Fighting for a region we need not have though ours by right it may be.... My India is wide enough, plenteous enough,
> Rich enough....
> We need no more. (17-18).

Zohra quotes religion while decrying the war why new lands? Why Kashmir? People here are of our faith I know, what matters who rules them so long as they bow to Islam? (19).

Prem Benn says, as she is proud of her son, fighting for his country:

> Proud am I that my son is fighting
> For such a prize. Lovely vale, had I've a Hundred sons.
> I, send them all to fight for thee and consider it.
> Scant sacrifice for such a treasure. (26)

This play assumes special significance in Indian situation especially in the post-Kargil scenario.

The dying of the sons is to be noted. Meenakshi's son dies a 'Satisfied young man' being his childhood ambition of flying in a plane got fulfilled. Kishore, Prem Behn's son, at his dying moments, craves that his life may be spared as he wants to drink life to its full. But he dies. Then there is poet who stabs himself in an emotional moment saying that in place of Kishore's life he is giving his life. This really puts questions before all who can think. The futility of war is apparent.

On the contrary, 'Meera' and 'Sita's Promise' set out to celebrate Indian art tradition and to acquaint the outsider about our culture tradition. No doubt Uma Parameswaran, through her "Meera;" a dance drama, proceeds from the familiar episodes in the life of Meera but an outsider has to stretch his imagination to grasp and comprehend the three roles given to Meera as Devki, Yasoda and finally as Radha, and Meera's faith in Krishna, her infinite love for Him.

It is owing to her infinite love for her Eternal lover Krishna that in Scene II, Meera takes herself for Devki; who brought forth the Child Divine. Through the myth of Krishna's birth, Parameswaran reveals to the Western world the spiritual grandeur and glorious culture of India.

In scene III Meera assumes the role of Yasoda, facing the boyish pranks, teasing the gopis and various mischiefs of her darling Krishna. Here the dramatist emphasises the mythical characters of Lord Krishna as saviour of mankind and destroyer of evil Kansa.

In the next scene of the play 'Meera' Krishna comes on earth to re-establish justice and protect the Universe as He declares in the 7th shlok of the 4th Chapter of Srimad Bhagvadgita.[3] In scene V Meera becomes Radha, drawing extreme satisfaction and delight in dancing with Krishna. Thus the three roles given to Meera—Devki, Yasoda and Radha symbolize the tireless effort of the finite to reach the infinite *i.e.* the final merging of the *atman* with the *Parmatman.*

'Sita's Promise' brings epic India closer to modern Canada through myth and dance. The play 'Sita's Promise' was written for the Arangetram of the first graduates when Uma's daughter was also one of those graduates. The play links epic India with modern Canada through myth and dance. She depicts the plight of the immigrants and the pangs of alienation symbolically by the sufferings of the bird. 'Sita's Promise' constitutes testimony to Uma Parameswaran's cultural rootedness. See how Sita promises, "I through my people shall surely come again and we shall build our temple and sing our songs with all the children to all the different countries who make this their home."[4]

The leading characters of this play, like the Ramayana, are Rama, Sita and Lakshman. But the plot is purely imaginative, full of bold digressions. Rama, the prince of Ayodhya was banished for 14 years and he leaves the kingdom with Sita and Lakshman. They travel far and wide, destroying the demons and helping sages and saints on the way. Sita's character here stands in sharp contrast to the ideal image of Sita as depicted in the Ramayan. Her remarks prove that she has followed Rama to the forest more for fun and enjoyment than out of her duty to her husband. Similarly the arguments of Lakshman with Rama also do not at all co-incide with the mythical character of Lakshman. Uma Parameswaran in 'Sita's Promise' concentrates on dance rather than on the mythical characters of the epic Ramayana. Her aim is to popularize Indian mythology as well as dance and music traditions among the Western countries. Really it is a highly commendable service to Indian drama and culture.

"Rootless but Green are the Boulevard Trees" depicts real life, the people in the different events, situations and experiences. The play centres around an East Indian family living in the suburbs of Winnipeg. The characters of the play belong to three generations:

> The First Generation—The parents, Sharad and Savitri Bhave—Shardd's Sister Veejata and her husband Anant Moghe.
>
> The Second Generation—The Bhave and Moghe Children.
>
> The Third Generation—The youngest siblings in their adolescent years—Krish Bhave (12), Priti Moghe (10).

Sharad Bhave, an atomic energy scientist in the India, had quitted and rots in Canada. His wife, Savitri, is a school teacher. She is more traditional than her husband. She strongly believes that "we carry our God within us and with us wherever we go." She wears saree inside the house, puts kumkum, looks after the needs of the family during the dining times, shows that she is still dominated by the Indian culture. Savitri is not worried about the loss of comforts. She struggles to keep her spirit alive. She is Indian in spirit but to certain extent she changes herself. She does not prevent her daughter Jyothi from dating as an Indian mother would have done, still she cannot allow the father to know the whereabouts of the daughter. So she deprives Jyothi of the usage of her mother's car but allows her to use her own.

The first generation who have spent most of their life in India and have settled in Canada in their middle ages, the conflict is not so intense as their roots are still in India. But the second generation suffer worse as they think Canada is their land, try to send roots and get assimilated. See a dialogue between the two:

Jayant : Our people, our old country, Dad, there's no, 'our people' and no 'old country' for anyone in the world anymore, least of all for us. This is our land and here we shall stay.

Sharad : Roots, son, roots. Can we really grow roots here?

Jayant : Sure Dad.[5] (34)

Thus throughout the play, Uma Parameswaran gives more importance to family bondage and emotional ties between the family members, the core of Indian culture. Jayant's giving up his idea of going out, Jyothi's refusal to date with Andre, Priti being consoled by Jayant and the happy family gathering at the end of the play, all go to prove not only Uma Parameswaran's cultural rootedness but the younger generation's strong footedness in their tradition.

Uma Parameswaran, as a writer, opts for the permanent exile abroad and yet continues to draw her cultural and aesthetic sustenance and substance from her Indian past. For one reason or other she continues to relate personally or vicariously to her homeland. As an expatriate writer, Uma attempts to 'grab the best of two worlds.' Most of her one-act plays recall an Indian past, with its mythology, legend and the gods and goddesses.

Now she is settled in Canada. She has been devoting much of her writing and efforts in the literary field to creating an identifiable South Asian Canadian Diaspora.

Another important writer in this field who deserves due attention is Manjula Padmanabhan. She was born in Delhi, grew up in Sweden, Pakistan, Thailand and now she is living in Delhi. She is a woman of versatile genius. She is well-known today as an artist, illustrator, cartoonist playwright and novelist. She has illustrated 21 children's books and has had a long running cartoon strip, 'Suki' in the *Sunday Observer* and later in *Pioneer*. Her cartoon strip, 'Suki' is also published as a book in the year 2001 and her etchings are featured in their own exhibition in Delhi.

Manjula Padmanabhan came into limelight by creating history when her pioneering play 'Harvest' won the first prize out of 1470 entries in 76 countries in 1997 in the first Onassis International Cultural Competition. 'Harvest' is a futuristic play about the sale of body parts and exploitative relations between developed and developing countries.

'Harvest' is the story of a miserable family dwelling in a pathetic condition of a chawl of Mumbai. Apart from money, many other social evils enveloping the society are also responsible for grim and tragic predicament and dehumanization of the city people. Om Prakash, a young man of twenty, under the pressure of compelling circumstances makes up his mind to become an organ donor and finally is bound to mortgage his body to a white First World buyer. This play is intellectual with the dominance of thought element, hence not quite suitable for stage performance.

This play brings into focus the cannibalistic society in which the sale of human organs has become a common practice. "Interplanta Services arrange for the sale and transplant of organs of willing Indians into the jaded bodied of rich Americans."[6] What name to be given to such type of slavery or compulsion? Such thought-provoking questions continue to ignite the mind of the audience.

Manjula Padmanabhan's recent play "Lights Out" presents a tragic spectacle of the daily rape of women, watched at a distance by the middle class characters. The victimized women like Leena and Naina cry for help but it goes unheeded by the men like Bhaskar and Mohan who try to quieten their conscience by arguing that the victims are after all only prostitutes, not decent women belonging to the dignified society.

Manjula Padmanabhan portrays a mean and moribund world where mothers sell their children for the 'price of rice.' Thus the themes of alienation and marginalization are the most recurrent in the works of Manjula Padmanabhan.

No doubt Indian English drama is a plant of poor growth owing to certain limitations, still we can predict a rich and fertile soil for the blooming and blossoming of the tree of Indian English drama. In fact there have been serious and sincere efforts for the theatre-oriented plays. The women playwrights have something distinct to offer to the audience. They have given new dimensions by infusing new type into this genre.

They are fully aware that the playwright is essentially a man of letters whose first commitment is to the truth. He/she has to unveil the truth which is hidden behind several layers. Theatricality cannot be a matter of technique only. The basic capability of playwright lies in the selection of the most appropriate and adequate slice of life to express his experience of truth. Women playwrights have proved through their plays that they fulfil the specific demands of theatre; as a play has music, dance and other art-forms too. They build their own world with conviction; they concentrate on theme and then the material is ready for presentation.

References

1. M. Dasan, "Writer as Fighter: Concern for Human Rights Violations in Mahasweta Devi's Play," *Flowering of Indian Drama Growth and Development*, ed. K. Venkata Reddy and R.K. Dhawan (New Delhi: Chaman Offset Press, 2004), 80.

2. *Ibid.*, 81-82.
3. यदा यदा हि धर्मस्य ग्लानिर्भवति भारत:
   अभ्युत्थानमधर्मस्य तदात्मानं सृजाम्यहम्।।

   Srimad Bhagvadgita, Chapter 4, Shlok 7.
4. Parameswaran, Uma, 'Rootless but Green are the Boulevard Trees' and 'Sita's Promise' in SACLIT Drama, Ed. Uma Parameswaran, IBH Prakashans, Bangalore, India, 1996, 87.
5. *Ibid.*, 34
6. Bijay Kumar Das, *Post Modern Indian English Literature* (New Delhi: Atlantic Publisher, 2003), 129.

BIBLIOGRAPHY

Abrams, M.H. *A Glossary of Literary Terms*. Madras: Macmillan & Co. Ltd., 1978.

Aiyer, K.V. *Kailasam Avara Smarane* ('Remembering Kailasam') Bangalore: Karnataka Sangh Central College, 1952.

Ambedkar, Dr. Babasaheb. *Writings and Speeches*. Bombay: Government of Maharashtra, 1987.

Anantha Murthy, U.R. "A Note on Karnad's *Hayavadana*." *Literary Criterion*, VIII, 4 (1978).

——. Introduction. *Tughlaq*. By Girish Karnad. Delhi: Oxford University Press, 1987, vii-x.

Annaiah Gowda, H.H. ed. *Indian Drama*, Mysore: University of Mysore, 1974.

Arora, Keval. "The Theatre in Translation." *Humanities Review*, 2.2 (1980).

Aurobindo, Sri. *Collected Plays and Short Stories*, Birth Centenary Library Popular Edition, Vols. 6 and 7. Pondicherry: Sri Aurobindo Ashram Trust, 1971.

Babu, Sarat M. "The Concept of Chastity and Naga Mandala," *The Plays of Girish Karnad: Critical Perspectives* ed. Jaydipsinh Dodiya. New Delhi: Prestige Books, 1999.

Bandyopadhyay, Samik. Introduction, *Ghashiram Kotwal* by Vijay Tendulkar. Trans. Jayant Karve and Eleanor Zelliot. Calcutta. Seagull, 1986, iii-ix.

Benegal, Som. *A Panorama of Theatre in India*. New Delhi: Indian Council for Cultural Relation, 1967.

Bentley, Eric. *In Search of Theatre.* New York: Vintage Books, 1953.

Bhatta, Krishna S. "Kailasam's English Plays" *Perspectives on Indian Drama in English* ed. M.K. Naik. Madras: Oxford University Press, 1977.

Bhattacharjee, Shampa. "Badal Sircar's *Street Plays*: A Thematic Study." Diss. Kakatiya U, 1994.

Boulos, Joseph N. "The Ramayana and the Aeneid: Some Salient Features," Meerut *Journal of Comparative Literature and Language* ed. T.R. Sharma, Vol. 5, No. 2, 1992.

Bowers, Faubion. *Theatre in the East.* New York: Thomas Nelson & Sons, 1956.

Chakraborty, A.K. "Foreword," *The Indian Imagination of Girish Karnad* by P. Dhanavel. New Delhi: Prestige Books, 2000.

Chatterjee, Kalika Ranja. "Philosophical Themes in Sri Aurobindo's Peruses the Deliverer," *Indian Writing in English* ed. Krishna Nandan Sinha. New Delhi: Heritage Publishers, 1979.

Cobin Martin. "A View of the Indian Theatre," Enact, 97 and 98 (Jan.-Feb., 1975), *Perspectives on Indian Drama in English* ed. M.K. Naik. Madras: Oxford University Press, 1977.

Coppala, Carlo. Foreword. *A Journal of South Asian Literature*, XIV 3-4 (1979), 89-90.

Currimbhoy, Asif. *The Complete Works of Asif Currimbhoy* ed. Faubion Bowers. New Delhi: I.B.H. Publishing House, 1970.

Dass, Veena Noble. "Experiment and Innovation in Modern Indian Drama in Translation: the Plays of Mohan Rakesh Badal Sircar, Vijay Tendulkar and Girish Karnad," *Contemporary Indian Drama* ed. Sudhakar Pandey and Freya Taraporewala. New Delhi: Prestige Books, 1990.

Desai, S.K. "Symbolism in the Plays of Rabindranath Tagore," *Critical Essays on Indian Writings in English* ed.

M.K. Naik, S.K. Desai and G.S. Amur. London: Macmillan, 1977.

Dev, Narendra. "Drama in Modern Bengal" *Drama in Modern India: The Writer's Responsibility in a Rapidly Changing World* ed. K.R. Srinivasa Iyengar, Bombay: P.E.N., 1961.

Dhanavel, P. *The Indian Imagination of Girish Karnad.* New Delhi: Prestige Books, 2000.

Dharwadker, Aparna. "Historical Fictions and Postcolonial Representation: Reading "Girish Karnad's *Tughlaq.*" PMLA, 110.1 (1995), 43-58.

Dhawan, R.K. "Girish Karnad: The Man and the Writer," *The Plays of Girish Karnad: Critical Perspectives* ed. Jaydipsinh Dodiya. New Delhi: Prestige Books, 1999.

Dhawan, R.K. ed. *Indian Literature Today.* 2 Vols. Delhi: Prestige Books, 1994.

Dodiya, Jayadipsinh ed. *The Plays of Girish Karnad: Critical Perspectives.* New Delhi: Prestige Books, 1999.

Dubey, Satyadev and Vijay Tendulkar. "Dialogue." *Gentleman,* Sept. 1983.

Dubey, Satyadev. "Introduction," Evan Indrajit, *Three Modern Indian Plays.* New Delhi: Oxford University Press, 1989.

Eakabaram, N. "Validity of Evan Indrajit: An Indian Version of an Absurd Play." *Essay in Criticism on Indian Literature in English.* Ed. M.S. Nagarajan et al. New Delhi: S. Chand, 1991.

Ezekiel, Nissim. *Three Plays* (Nalini Marriage, Poem and Sleepwalkers). Calcutta: Writers Workshop, 1969.

Fergusson, Franci. *Theldea of Theatre.* Princeton: Princeton University Press, 1949.

Flickinger, Roy C. *The Greek Theatre and its Drama.* Chicago: Chicago University Press, 1961.

Gargi, Balwant. *Theatre in India.* New York: Theatre Arts, 1962.

George, K.M., ed. *Comparative Indian Literature.* Madras: Macmillan, 1984.

Ghose, Sisir Kumar. *Rabindranath Tagore*. New Delhi: Sahitya Academi, 1986.

Gowda, Anniah. *Indian Drama*. Mysore: University of Mysore, 1974.

Granville-Barker, H. *The Use of Drama*. London: Sidewick and Jackson, 1947.

Gupta, Chandra Bhan. *The Indian Theatre*. Banaras: Motilal Banarasidass, 1954.

Gupta, Santosh. "Naga-Mandala: A Story of Marriage and Love," *The Plays of Girish Karnad: Critical Perspectives* ed. Jaydipsinh Dodiya. New Delhi: Prestige Books, 1999.

Iyengar, K.R. Srinivasa. *Indian Writing in English*. New Delhi: Sterling Publisher Private Limited, 1987.

Jacob, George C. "Myth as Fulcrum: Lord Ganesh as Dramatic Presence in Hayavadana," *The Plays of Girish Karnad: Critical Perspective* ed. Jaydipsinh Dodiya. New Delhi: Prestige Books, 1999.

Jacobus, Lee A. *The Bedford Introduction to Drama*. New York: St. Martin's Press, 1989.

Jaganmohan Chari, A. and E. Renuka. "The Plays of Vijay Tendulkar." *New Quest*, Jan.-Feb. 1988, 27-37.

Jha, Vivek Dutta. "Mohan Rakesh and his plays" Encat, Jan.-Feb. 1973, no page. Lal, Ananda "Form Spartacus to Quo Vadis? Bengali Theatre." *Telegraph*, 24 June 1988.

Joshi, R.G. *Myth in Indian Drama*. Delhi: B.R., n.d.

Joshipura, Pranav. "Naga-Mandala Reconsidered," *The Plays of Girish Karnad: Critical Perspectives* ed. Jaydipsinh Dodiya. New Delhi: Prestige Books, 1999.

Kailasam, T.P. *Fulfilment*. Bangalore: B.S. Rama Rao, 1933.

——. Keechaka (Retold by B.S. Rama Rao). Bangalore: Chhaya Publisher, 1949.

——. *Little Lays and Plays* (1933). rpt. Bangalore: B.S. Rama Rao, 1964.

——. *The Burden*. Bangalore: B.S. Rama Rao, 1933.

——. *The Curse of Karna* (Karna: The Brahmin's Curse). Madhava & Sons, 1946.

——. *The Purpose*. Bangalore: Madhava & Sons, 1944.

——. *Tollugatti*, Bangalore: B.S. Rama Rao, 1965.

Kale, M.R. ed. *The Mrcchakatika of Sudraka*. Varanasi: Motilal Banarsidass, 1972.

Kale, Manohar. *Bhartiya Natya Saundarya*. Delhi: Megha Prakashan, 1982.

Kale, Pramod. *The Theatric Universe* (A Study of the Natyashastra). Bombay: Popular Prakashan, 1974.

Karnad, Girish. "Interview." Indian Cinema Super Bazaar. ed. Aruna Vasudev and Philip Lengeet.

——. *Hayavadana*. Chennai: Oxford University Press, 1997.

——. *Naga-Mandala*. Delhi: Oxford University Press, 1997.

——. *Tale-Danda*. New Delhi: Ravi Dayal, 1993.

——. *Tughlaq*. Delhi: Oxford University Press, 1987.

——. *Yayati* (Hindi trans.) B.R. Narayana. Delhi: Saraswati Vihar, 1979.

Krishna Bhatta, S. "Indo-English Women Playwrights." *Triveni*, 49.1 (1980), 39-46.

——. *Indian English Drama: A Critical Study*. New Delhi: Sterling, 1987.

Kulkarni, S.S. "The Plays of Sri Aurobindo", *Perspectives on Indian Drama in English* ed. M.K. Naik. Madras: Oxford University Press, 1977.

Kurtkoti, Kirtinath. "Introduction" to *Hayavadana*. Chennai: Oxford University Press, 1997.

Levi, Sylvain. *The Theatre of India*. Trans. Mukherji Narayan. 2 Vols. Calcutta: Writers Workshop, 1978.

Lukacs, George. "The Sociology of Modern Drama" trans. Lee Baxandell. *The Theory of the Modern Stage* ed. Eric Bently Middlesex: Penguin Books Ltd., 1968.

Maharishi, Mohan. "Changing Role of Words in Theatre: Mohan Rakesh." Sangeet Natak, 22 (1971), 19-27.

Mukherji, Nirmal. "The Plays of Rabindranath Tagore," *Perspectives on Indian Drama in English* ed. M.K. Naik, Madras; Oxford University Press, 1977.

Nagpal, Kavita. "The Badal Sircar Magic." *The Hindustan Times*, 5 April 1992, 13.

Naik, G.H. "Karnad's *Tughlaq*." Enact, 193-94 (1983).

Naik, M.K. ed. *A History of Indian English Literature*. New Delhi: Sahitya Academi, 1982.

——. *Dimensions of Indian English Literature*. New Delhi: Sterling Publishers Private Limited, 1984.

——. *Perspectives on Indian Drama in English*. Madras: Oxford University Press, 1977.

Nandakumar, Prema. "Perseus the Deliver," *Perspectives on Indian Drama in English* ed. M.K. Naik. Madras: Oxford University Press, 1977.

Nicoll, Allardyce. *The Theatre of Dramatic Theory*. Bristol: George G. Harrap & Co. Ltd., 1962.

——. *World Drama*. London: George G. Harrap & Co. Ltd., 1959.

Nigam, R.L. "Adhe Adhure: A comment." Enact, 32-33 (1969).

Pandey, Sudhakar & Freya Taraporewala ed. *Contemporary Indian Drama*. New Delhi: Prestige Books, 1990.

Parameswaran, Uma. *Sons, Must Die and Other Plays*. New Delhi: Prestige Books, 1998.

Paul, Rajinder. "Girish Karnad Interviewed," *Point of View* ed. K.K. Sharma, Vol. 1, Summer 1994.

——. "Modern India Theatre." *Seminar*, 359 (1989), 39-42.

Radha, Kironomy. *Bengali Theatre*. New Delhi: National Book Trust, India, 1978.

Rai, R.N. *Theory of Drama: Comparative Study of Aristotle and Bharata*. New Delhi: Classical Publishing Company, 1992.

Rajaratnam, G.P. Kailasam Nenapu Kailasam Kathana, R.A. Malagi. "The Curse of Karna," *Perspectives on*

Indian Drama in English ed. M.K. Naik. Madras: Oxford University Press, 1977.

Ramamurthi, K.S. "Indian Drama in English with special reference to *Tughlaq*." *Litt. Crit.* 5.1 (1979), 922.

Rangacharya, Adya. "Classical Indian Drama and Modern Indian Theatre," *Indian Drama* ed. H.H. Annaiah Gowda. Mysore: University of Mysore, 1974.

——. *The Indian Theatre*. New Delhi: Sahitya Akademi, 1971.

Raykar, Subhangi S. "The Development of Girish Karnad as Dramatist: Hayavadana," *The Plays of Girish Karnad: Critical Perspectives* ed. Jaydipsinh Dodiya. New Delhi: Prestige Books, 1999.

Reddy, P. Bayapa. *Studies in Indian Writing in English*. New Delhi: Prestige Books, 1990.

——. *The Plays of Asif Currimbhoy*. Calcutta: Writers Workshop, 1985.

Singh, Amritjit. "Contemporary Indo-English Literature: An Approach," *Aspects of Indian Writing in English* ed. M.K. Naik. Madras: Macmillan & Co. Ltd., 1979.

Sinha, A.K. *The Dramatic Art of Sri Aurobindo*. Delhi: S. Chand & Co. Ltd., 1979.

Sinha, K.N. ed. *Indian Writing in English*. New Delhi: Heritage Publishers, 1979.

Sircar, Badal. *Evam Indrajit, Three Modern Indian Plays* (Tughlaq, Evam Indrajit & Silence! The Court is in Session). New Delhi: Oxford University Press, 1999.

——. *The Third Theatre*. Calcutta: Sircar, 1978. Articles, Dissertations, Interviews and Introductions.

Sundararaman, M.N. "Tradition and Modernity in Indian English Drama," *The Journal of Indian Writing in English*, 21.1 (1993): 1-13.

Suneel Seema. "Karnad's *Yayati* Reconsidered," *The Plays of Girish Karnad: Critical Perspectives* ed. Jaydipsinh Dodiya. New Delhi: Prestige Books, 1999.

Tagore, Rabindranath. *Chitra*. New Delhi: Macmillan, 1980.

——. *Sacrifice and Other Plays*. Madras: Macmillan, 1985.

Thompson, Edward. *Rabindranath Tagore*. London: Oxford University Press, 1948.

Vatsyayan, Kapila. *Traditional Indian Theatre: Multiple Streams*. New Delhi: National Book Trust, India, 1980.

Venkatesan, K. "Badal Sircar's Third Theatre." Diss. S.K.U., 1993.

Verghese, Paul C. *Problems of the Indian Creative Writer in English*. Bombay: Somaiya Publications Pvt. Ltd., 1971.

Wasi, Jehanara. "New Trail in Marathi Theatre" *Link*, 1 Oct. 1989, 36.

CONTRIBUTORS

Supriya Shukla, Head Dept. of English, V.S.S.D. College, Kanpur, Uttar Pradesh.

R.N. Rai, Prof. of English, Banaras Hindu University, Varanasi, Uttar Pradesh.

Vinod Bala Sharma, Prof. of English, Mata Sundari College for Women, University of Delhi, New Delhi.

Alka Saxena, Senior Reader in English, D.A.V. College, Civil Lines, Kanpur, Uttar Pradesh.

Neeru Tandon, Senior Reader, V.S.S.D. College, Kanpur, Uttar Pradesh.

N.M. Nigam, Head Dept. of English, Mahila Mahavidyala, Kidwai Nagar, Kanpur, Uttar Pradesh.

Anupam Shukla, Head Dept. of English, Dayanand Anglo Vedic College, Civil Lines, Kanpur, Uttar Pradesh.

M.R. Verma, Department of English, Gurukul Kangri University, Haridwar, Uttaranchal.

Sanjay Kumar Swarnakar, Asstt. Prof. of English, C.S.J.M.U., Kalyanpur, Kanpur, Uttar Pradesh.

Madhumita Ganguli, Senior Reader in English, Christ-Church College, The Mall, Kanpur, Uttar Pradesh.

Jaya Kapoor, A.N.D. M.M.V., Harsh Nagar, Kanpur, Uttar Pradesh.

Priya Srivastava, D.A.V. College, Civil Lines, Kanpur, Uttar Pradesh.

R.P. Pradhan, V.S.S.D. College, Nawabganj, Kanpur, Uttar Pradesh.

Nivedita Tandon, Dayanand Girls College, Civil Lines, Kanpur, Uttar Pradesh.

B.R. Agrawal, Mahila Mahavidyala, P.G. College, Kidwai Nagar, Kanpur, Uttar Pradesh.

Reshu Shukla, V.S.S.D. College, Kanpur, Uttar Pradesh.

Anshul Chandra, V.S.S.D. College, Kanpur, Uttar Pradesh.

Indulekha Roy Burman, D.G. College, Civil Lines, Kanpur, Uttar Pradesh.

Anjana Trivedi, Head Dept. of English, Vidya Mandir Girls Degree College, Swaroop Nagar, Kanpur, Uttar Pradesh.

B/182